DADLESS...

...BUT NOT FATHERLESS

BRENDON LENNON

First published by The Rural Publishing Company 2023

Copyright © Brendon Lennon 2023

Print: 978-0-6484431-7-9
eBook: 978-0-6484431-8-6

This work is copyright. Apart from any use permitted under the *Copyright Act 1968*, no part of this publication may be reproduced, stored in a retrieval system or transmitted in any form or by any means, electronic, mechanical, photocopying, recording or otherwise, without the prior written permission of Brendon Lennon.

The information in this book is based on the author's experiences and opinions. The author and publisher disclaim responsibility for any adverse consequences, which may result from use of the information contained herein. Permission to use any external content has been sought by the author. Any breaches will be rectified in further editions of the book.

Cover Design: The Rural Publishing Company

Layout and Typesetting: The Rural Publishing Company

The Rural Publishing Company
Email: hello@theruralpublishingcompany.com.au
Website: https://theruralpublishingcompany.com.au/

CONTENTS

PART 1: DADLESS 11
    CHAPTER 1: IN A NUTSHELL 12
    CHAPTER 2: POINTS OF STRUGGLE 15
        1. Rejection 16
        2. Not fitting in 19
        3. Unforgiveness / Resentment 20
        4. Performance / Commitment 21
        5. Confidence 24
        6. Fear of Others' Opinions & Words 26
        7. Faulty Thinking 28
        8. Character 31
    CHAPTER 2: TYPES OF DADS 36
        Which of these 'dads' fits your experience? 37
    CHAPTER 3: MY PROCESS 39
        My Justification 39
    CHAPTER 4: A PERSONAL PERSPECTIVE 70
        My Will and Emotion 73
        A Small Sidestep 77
        My Commitment 81
        Transition Can Be Tough 85
        Expect a Fight 87
        My Thoughts and Words 89

CHAPTER 5: BE WATCHFUL 93

CHAPTER 6: GOING FORWARD 95

CHAPTER 7: LEARNING FROM GOD IN DIFFICULT TIMES 98

CHAPTER 8: WHY ARE SOME DADS GOOD AND OTHERS BAD? 120

    Humanity 123
    The Man 127

CHAPTER 9: THE DADLESS EFFECT ON CHILDREN 132

CHAPTER 10: SO WHERE TO FROM HERE? 135

PART 2: ...BUT NOT FATHERLESS 137

CHAPTER 11: GOD IS FATHER 138

CHAPTER 12: GOD IS A FATHER TO THE FATHERLESS 140

CHAPTER 13: WHAT DOES IT MEAN TO BE PART OF GOD'S FAMILY? 142

    Adopted 142
    Recognition and Privilege 143
    Personal Responsibilities 143
    Walking in the Spirit 145
    Being Holy 147
    We are favoured/blessed 148
    Being In His Plan 149

CHAPTER 14: HOW IS GOD A FATHER TO ME? 153

    He First Loved / Chose Me 153
    His Timing Is Perfect 156
    He Protects Me 157
    My Character Development / He is Gracious 160
    He Guides Me 165
    His Word 177

He Never Leaves Me..182
His Goodness / Kindness.. 185
His Faithfulness 192
He Disciplines / Teaches... 195
His Presence 202
He Encourages 211
His Fatherheart..217

CHAPTER 15: THE LAST PAGE WITH MY DAD............................221

CHAPTER 16: NEW BEGINNINGS AND NEW HORIZONS 233

No Season Lasts Forever..233
A New Start..234
God, The Mechanic & Body Repairer of Life 237
Some Last Thoughts 239

THANK YOU

First, I want to thank my wife, Carmel. For your ongoing support and encouragement to me, not only during this whole time in writing this book but for over the last thirteen years as my wife and best friend. You make me a better man, and I am thankful that I have been blessed with you and have been blessed by you. Love you, baby.

I would also like to thank my mum (Chicky). You had to wear many hats as you worked hard and painstakingly over many years to give myself, Jim and Brad your best. You always encouraged me with your sincere words. You helped shape me with your values, virtues, and courage to be a good person. As hard as things were, you always ensured we had enough and were looked after. You are a woman of wisdom and constancy. I look up to you. Thank You for believing in me and loving me. Love you, mum.

Most importantly, I want to thank Father God for saving me and continually giving me the grace to live and be an encouragement to others. I want to thank You for giving me this opportunity to write this book to help others succeed. Thank You for giving me my wonderful son Isaac, a son of promise, so I also know what it is like to be a father. I am grateful to be a husband, a dad, and, most importantly, your son. Thank You for showing me love and teaching me what is right and worth pursuing. Thank you for showing me how to be a better dad and how to live as an honoring son.

Lastly, I want to thank all of you who have spoken into my life over the years and gone over and above to help shape and solidify my godly character into my life. Thank you all.

INTRODUCTION

We each live different lives, but no matter who you are, we all have needs. We all have physical bodies that need food, water and protection. We also need a sense of love, value, safety and security. What is life without these? What brings you a sense of worth, purpose, a sense of belonging or identity? What is your purpose in life? Do you have a sense of feeling lost or feel that you're in no man's land? Where do you come from? Where are you headed in life? What is your game plan? Do you have a personal vision for your life? Do you know your life's purpose? Do you believe there is hope for you, or is it too late?

These questions will impact your life in one way or another. On top of that, growing up without a complete and imperfect family unit is like a massive boulder thrown into your lake of life, where the ripples are still causing you fallout. The way you react, the way you see things, the way you carry yourself, speak with people, how you treat them, your attitudes about life, judgments you make about yourself and others. These and many other examples can stem from at least one thing you and I may have in common; we missed out on having a dad in our lives, being 'Dadless.'

Have you ever felt ripped off and had no one there to show you the ropes of life and how to deal with things as they come up? Or, being despised or laughed at just because you didn't have a dad? You were judged inferior simply because there was a 'lack' in your life. Did you, or do you still blame yourself for not having a dad? Do you blame your mother for your situation?

Do you still have that sting of not having someone you wanted to be your hero in your life? Do you still crave that? Or perhaps none of this means anything to you? Let me tell you something, you and I are incredibly and deeply affected by the lack of a dad in our lives, regardless of your position.

You may be young, at school, college, university, or a working person; whatever your situation, you may be older with your own family. Wherever you are in life, and when you don't have a dad, it will affect you in many ways. You may feel that you want to get on track because your past has derailed you. You have been left dadless for whatever reason and that is not on you. You were knocked off course and have been off course for so long that you don't even realise it or notice it.

Everything seems fine and normal to you. But is it really the normal you were meant to have? What other normal could there be? You might be saying to yourself, 'I'm doing ok in life; I'm working a good job, I'm with a good woman/man, I even have my own family, and I'm happy with that. Life is not a perfect painting, but I'm doing well, all things considered'.

Maybe your life has been one of strife, trouble, loss, grief and struggle with addiction, violence, or abuse, times in and out of jail, foster care, rehab, and dangerous situations. Or maybe you were left holding the bag, with all the responsibility a dad should have taken on. It has been a trainwreck for as long as you can remember, and this is your 'normal.'

INTRODUCTION

So, do all these life events come from not having a dad? No, but as we go through life, we sometimes make decisions that hurt ourselves and others. We don't always know the better choices or direction to go in. That said, if you make a course correction, your past is not necessarily your pathway to destruction. It is true that in life, you go where your choices take you. I'm saying that your history impacts how you do life now and potentially in your future. I'm saying that life may not have always been good, but realising it or not, my life, your life, has been affected in ways that have been historically, sometimes out of reach of our understanding. I hope that you will gain some understanding and knowledge throughout these pages.

Whichever side of the coin you are on, life can be better, internally and externally, for your soul and your surroundings. It's time to understand who you are, where you come from, why you are headed in the direction you are heading, why you do the things you do and feel the way you do, and how and what you think.

The absence of a dad fractured my life. I want a hero in my life, one I can look up to, rely on, and correct me when I'm off course. Someone to build me up, bolster my self-worth and identity, and give me confidence, strength, and solid character. Someone to show me how to handle situations with life experience, to show respect to women and others. Someone to teach me how to be productive and an example for me.

I would have loved having a dad in my life to show me how to camp, go fishing, be challenging and resilient, but at the same time, be understanding and show me compassion and what it means to be accountable and have integrity.

It would have been awesome to have a dad who could show me how to drive, fight (stand up for myself), play pool, and just hang out to do all kinds of dad/son stuff, build things and hone skills. Over the years, I have acquired all these skills to varying degrees of success. And while it is true that you can attain these things in your life by yourself, having a dad present to take and guide you through these ventures would potentially have made a massive difference to you.

Unfortunately, I never got those chances and opportunities with my dad, which is likely to be the same for you too.

Irrespective that our lives may have been different, there are underlying matters of the heart and soul that may be similar. At this writing, I am 47 years old, and still, to this day, I desire a physical dad in my life. But at this stage in the game, it's too late for that. If you are of the age where you understand that there is a longing in your heart and desire in your soul to have a dad or have one at all to simply set things right in your own life, there is absolute assurance and resolve for you to get. While there is life, there is hope.

The whole purpose of this book is to relate to you by my own experience, to come alongside you and help you recognise and make the change/s necessary for breakthrough and fruitfulness to come into your life and situation. Our lives may be different, but we have at least one major thing in common, we both need to resolve the dad issue in our life because it affects us so deeply and significantly, our whole experience and expression are altered as a direct result of our dadless history.

You might have had a dadless past, but you don't have to have a fatherless future.

INTRODUCTION

I have had to go through many things and deal with the aftermath of not having a dad in my life, but I will say; I have made progress through the process. And it has taken me years, but I trust this will not be as lengthy as it has been for me to see you get through your process.

We may be dadless, but we are not fatherless. I will explain this in full.

This reality for me, has changed my whole life. I know it can be the same for you as well. I know it! Let's go on a road trip together, as both the journey and the destination are well worth it.

At the end of specific sections in this book, I will give you things to help get you on your way to your destination. Remember, it's _your_ road trip to restoration; I'm just here to help get you on your way. I trust that my life experiences and hands-on approach will get real results and breakthroughs for you too.

My only disclaimer is that I'm sharing my own personal circumstances, my responses to those situations, and the personal outcomes I have observed and experienced during my journey. I am not a health professional. I expect that at least one or possibly more of these individual applications will positively and permanently impact your life.

Now let's get down to business.

Let me ask you a question. What does it mean to be dadless, but not fatherless?

First, there is the easy-to-explain physical dad who gave you your physical start. Then there is the second not-as-easy-to-explain spirit father, who gives you your spiritual and eternal beginning. Your biological dad gave you your initial physical birth, while your spirit dad, Father God, gives you a fresh and new start in life.

It's also timely and intentional that you are reading this book now. I believe that the building you are currently in, or the tree you are now under while reading these words, were established there intentionally. The building did not get there on its own; the tree was not planted there by accident. Your very surroundings have been carefully and creatively conceived intentionally and consciously. You are reading this book for a reason. I am conveying to you with a purpose that, together with my experience and your participation, you will get closer to your destination.

I'll say this here: God (the dad of Jesus) is a **'Father to the fatherless...'** - Psalm 68:5. This effectively includes the entire human race, but it is true on a personal level just as much.

I'm going to tell you how he is a father, how he got me through tough times, how he taught me things and how he showed me what a father is really like. He filled the emptiness in my life very well and he wants to do the same for you too. He can get you to that place you need to be. Give him a chance now. You won't be disappointed in him.

The only things you will lose will be heartache, unforgiveness, negative thinking and all those other destructive things and thoughts you may currently endure on a personal level that affects your everyday living. You will only gain. God's help and

INTRODUCTION

trust in my personal accounts will hopefully help demonstrate this reality for you.

As you and I have our own personal experiences and life lessons, we each differ in our stories to share and in relating to others. My own experiences, like yours, are our own and are unique. I am going to share with you some of my situations and outcomes that I believe will help you on your way to becoming a man of mettle.

Ok, let's do this.

PART 1: DADLESS...

CHAPTER 1: IN A NUTSHELL

I must start by sharing brief parts of my life and how it was for me, particularly in my teens and through my twenties, thirties and forties. As I understand it, my dad left us (my mum and two other brothers) when I was around 18 months old, with much debt. Not a good start for anyone.

My first memory of him was when I was seven years of age; mum said, 'You're meeting someone special today.' So, as I remember, this tall, skinny man in an old, beige panel van visited us for a day. Later I found out that he was my dad. Since I was probably so young, I didn't think too much of that occasion at the time. It was normal not to have him around, so I didn't know any different. It wasn't until I was in my late teens that I saw him again for an afternoon.

You see, he lived up north of the country in and around Cape York, the top end of Queensland. We lived down in southern New South Wales in a little town called Culcairn, three and a half thousand kilometers away (over 2,000 miles).

By the time I met him the second time, he had another partner and three kids. Which means I have two full brothers (one of which I am a twin, the younger), two other half-brothers, and one half-sister. Since then, I have met my eldest half-brother and sister only once. We sometimes keep in contact via social media.

PART 1: DADLESS...

But even from the first moment I met Mick (my dad) until now, I have never in my recollection had the desire to go and see him and get to know him. People over the years asked me if I was interested in seeing him, and I said, 'No, not really, he's just another face in the crowd to me; I don't feel anything for him.'

I also recall only one phone call with him, which merely lasted a minute or two. But that's all there has been as far as the communication between us, until recently. When I saw him in my late teens, he told us boys that he hadn't taken responsibility for leaving. Regardless, he still didn't really explain anything to us or give us a valid reason (if there is one). During that conversation he spoke the entire time with a slight smile on his face (it seemed) as if to communicate to us that he really didn't care. It was like he was saying 'Hey, sorry for not turning up to the game today; no big deal, maybe next time.' That's all I remember of that meeting, other than that he came down because he was buying a new car.

The impact the absence of a dad had on me was significant. Growing up, it showed that, especially with my twin and I, it seemed we were easy targets from other boys in the town (who of course had dads) of being picked on, bullied, judged, scorned and ganged up on.

These things happened from time to time, just like it would have for many kids, but as a result I felt defenseless, rejected, insecure, judged, resentful and weak, with little confidence and a sense of feeling average at best.

Let me say that feelings and emotions were not the only things affected. They're only part of the story. How I saw myself, my general performance, how I related to others, my confidence level, my insecurities and how I measured up with others all played a part in how I looked at and lived life.

You may be thinking to yourself, 'This guy is fragile; harden up princess!' Well, let's take a look at the following list, and like me, mark the points you struggle with.

CHAPTER 2: POINTS OF STRUGGLE

I had a variety of aspects that I struggled with. These include:

1. **Rejection**: He didn't want me, so I don't want him.
2. **Not fitting in:** A perception/feeling of being on the outer.
3. **Unforgiveness / Resentment**: I don't care for him. What he did to me was unforgivable and I resent him for what he did and didn't do.
4. **Performance / Commitment:** I was never encouraged, corrected, pushed, directed, stretched or motivated when needed. I did the minimum, settled for second best and didn't complete most things I started.
5. **Confidence**: I was not bold, courageous, daring or assertive in whatever I did. I was nervous and afraid. I had no fire in the belly or steel in my back.
6. **Fear of Others' Opinions and Words**: What will they think? What will they say?
7. **Faulty Thinking:** I'm average at best. I'm less valuable and less important than others. I am inferior. There is something wrong with me. I am weak. I have nothing to offer. I am shallow.
8. **Character**: I didn't do what I said. I am inconsistent. Unreliable. Not dependable. I'm a quitter.

I'll share more detail about how these points impacted me and still, and to a point, have a residual effect on my life today. I must add, The Lord has been faithful and good to me, and I have come a long way from the impacts that these issues have had on my life, and I am nowhere near where I was from the effect and power upon my life they once had.

So, let's dive a little deeper.

1. Rejection

I have felt rejection for as long as I can remember. I only knew this to be my reality in life, so feeling and thinking anything else was unknown and foreign. I guess I just lived with it. Living and thinking that 'fractured/broken' was my normal.

When someone seemed interested in me or showed that they cared, I was immediately drawn to them. It meant a truck load to me that someone saw me and went out of their way to talk to me or to just want to hang out. But I could always spot a fake. I knew when someone talked to me but they weren't really caring or interested. Heck, they often didn't even give me eye contact.

This always left a negative thought in my mind and a slight hardening of my heart with emotion towards those people. I wasn't expecting every person I met to want to be best mates. From that, my thinking was; if you are not going to be sincere, don't talk to me at all. I remember guarding myself to avoid getting too close to others and putting myself out there and risking feeling or being rejected again.

Today, though, I don't feel the risk is so significant. Quite minor, actually. Even to the point of not coming up on the radar. Still, I wouldn't say I like the feeling or thought of being rejected (no one does really), but I have grown. I'm also accepted by the people close to me and, of course, Father God. He accepts me no matter what, so I feel more solid and secure.

When I first came to the Lord, I was somewhat broken, a sinner. Over the years, I have seen the faithfulness of God and His love and care for me come through time and again.

'But if we confess our sins to Him, He is faithful and just to forgive us our sins and to cleanse us from all unrighteousness.'
- 1 John 1:9.

I have also learned something else that is very important. And that is sometimes when I feel or perceive that I believe that I have been rejected; in reality, this is often not necessarily the case. Because I don't know their current situation or emotional state, it's simply a judgement or perception.

What was common for me earlier on from my imperfect and limited perspective was that I would judge a situation, comment or response from others and take it as though they had rejected me as a person. Or, in a group conversation, I would volunteer my opinion on something and no one seemed interested in my experience on a topic which challenged me and my sense of worth. My **misunderstanding/misinterpretation** of a situation or person has caused me to put on the rejection hat. And this affected my relationships. My good wife and I have had many conversations about this, and she has shown me that not every person, comment, action or response has been one of rejection towards me. She has helped me to see things from a more accurate and correct position. And this has helped me a lot.

Misunderstandings / Misinterpretations are the mothers of many unnecessary, unreliable and unfounded responses. These can cause lots of issues to arise and both stifle and hinder already solid relationships. The word of God says that the renewing of our mind transforms us. We become a different person over time through the new things we think and take hold of in our minds. The Bible also teaches us to **'Fix your (our) thoughts on what is true, and honourable, and right, pure, lovely and admirable. Think about things that are excellent and worthy of praise.'** - Philippians 4:8.

Another thought I want to make is that when we dwell on rejection, it is normally about ourselves. This can be unhealthy, but it's so easy to do. And while we're looking at ourselves, we're not looking at the one who can take us out of our situation to attain that proper perspective. The road is different for everyone, but I know from personal experience that God can somehow take away the hurtful side effects of rejection, bring healing, and restore us to complete wholeness. I would say to you now, that declaring God's living and powerful word over your life out loud, frequently, will have a powerful effect on your life. Scriptures like:

'I will never leave nor forsake you.' - Hebrews 13:5.

'But God demonstrates His own love toward us, in that while we were still sinners, Christ died for us.' - Romans 5:8.

'Keep me as the apple of Your eye.' - Psalms 17:8.

'The Lord says, 'I will guide you along the best pathway for your life. I will advise you and watch over you.' - Psalm 32:8.

PART 1: DADLESS...

What I glean from these Scriptures is that I'm not on my own, I was worth dying for, I am special in His opinion, and that He promises to guide and direct me through my entire life. He cares for me no matter what. No rejection here!

God will turn your hardest battle into your greatest victory!

2. Not fitting in

A significant point of contention for me. For my whole life, I have always felt a sense or thought I was on the fringes of any group, event, club or circle of friends. Even within the church, I always felt that I just didn't fit in. I have always struggled with this. Though in my previous church, where I was quite engaged and rubbing shoulders with leadership and youth, being on the church board, being responsible for running the church while my senior pastor was away, preaching and hosting various services and occasions for many years, I constantly felt somewhat like a 'square peg in a round hole' with these facets of my life. It's not like I didn't have a sense of fulfillment, satisfaction, or even purpose; I just felt and thought that I was amongst it but not entirely 'part' of it.

This would explain to me, in part anyway, why I sometimes feel loneliness, sadness or even depression symptoms. At times I feel isolation and sadness and then this often develops into a somewhat moderate level of depression, momentarily. Not experiencing a life of 'belonging' from my dad may have extended over into my experience with other people throughout the years with friendships that I have made but am no longer with as I have moved away to another location. Forging new friendships and being part of new groups with new people has never been easy, but these are factors that helped me to grow and helped me avoid becoming stuck within myself.

I recall one time at work when one of the other 'additional support' workers I was working with asked the client if they were interested in playing a game of cards, to which the client replied, 'I don't like card games.' The support worker then said, 'That's because you haven't played the right game yet.'

Finding the right group, club or interest, or fulfilling your personal dream will be life-changing for you. I have realised that getting with the right circle or group of people with the same interests and values helped me get away from my thoughts and roadblocks, improved my life, and benefited those around me too. I can then become a more productive and fruitful person who does likewise.

Also, changing what I think (most importantly) and talking things out with my wife (or someone you can trust and grow from) has helped me work through things and become a better person.

3. Unforgiveness / Resentment

When you say, 'I hate you!' you're actually saying, 'You hurt me!' I grew up not knowing my dad, and this was my life. But as I got older, I noticed a growing resentment towards him for what he did/didn't do. He left us with no commitment to come back. History has certainly proven that. But what I started to notice more and more was my snowballing resentment toward him. This was an underlying problem for me for many years and it was getting bigger. I guess I had been a Christian for quite a number of years and started to realise that I needed to do something about this personal issue I was struggling with.

I was beginning to take on some responsibilities with my church and I started to know who this God was and what Jesus did for me. So, with my mouth, I was saying good and positive things to God and to others, but with my heart and thoughts, I was saying much the opposite about my dad. This was somewhat hypocritical. This was difficult for me because the resentment I was trying to deal with was deeply entrenched in my soul. I got some counselling over the years but still had this underlying problem I was struggling to resolve. It was stubborn.

So, after a long time, I saw that I had resented him for leaving, but there was also resentment for the excuse he gave and how he said it. And what was also developing over the years was the fact that I was starting to get agitated about the fact that this resentment was still there even after all these decades had passed – what a predicament. I have had to say many times over the years that I forgive him and repent to the Lord of my unforgiveness and resentment towards my dad.

The bottom line is that now I have come to the place where I am resentment free towards my dad – what a breakthrough! I have come a long way and it is only with God's loving grace and patience and how He has dealt with me over the years that I have been able to come this far in my journey. But for me at this point in my life, I can honestly say my issue is resolved and I am the better for it. I pray that he will ultimately come to know Father God just as I have. But more on this point later.

4. Performance / Commitment

I have commenced numerous things over my life and have noticed over time I started more things than I finished. And my performance level could have been much more. Whether it was going to the gym, being involved with martial arts, studying or giving my best to whatever it was, I had started. I also saw a widespread practice/habit as well; and that was when I was asked if I could be part of something, help out or to come along to an event or occasion; I would normally say 'Yes,' but I would often usually end up saying 'No' right at the last moment. Quite annoying for the other party. I saw for myself and felt that I was doing life on low level performance and commitment.

I believe things might have been somewhat different having someone there for me to motivate and model to me, at the very least, some level of grit, tenacity and commitment. Over the years, I found myself in many very short-term relationships and not always for the right reasons. I would ask myself at times, when in a relationship that I knew I was never meant to be in; 'How did I get here?', 'Why am I in this?'

This happened time and time again, but I was fighting a battle I was not equipped for. I didn't realise this until I was in my early 30s. Even being a Christian for about 20 years, I still struggled with the same issues, such as performance, commitment and recurring patterns of getting into short-term relationships, to name a few.

Over the years, I have done many things of which I am proud and have a good sense of achievement, but there was a problem that I had to deal with that was bugging me no end. The Holy Spirit had brought me to a place where I could deal with and put certain battles behind me. In some respects, I had been mirroring my dad's kind of lifestyle. There were elements of noncommittal, drifting and seemingly casual and average Achievement.

Now my dad was not the cause of everything I had done because I made my choices; however, the 'example' set before me was one I tended to mimic and, at some point, live out unconsciously. There was also the reality of spiritual legality and power that I was contending with, but I had no idea they played a part in my struggles.

You see, being a Christian is very much a legal matter. The Devil has a legal right over your life; you are not protected when you are not in Christ. When the blood of Jesus redeems you of all your sin and guilt, you are declared righteous; without sin, you are innocent of all charges.

'There is therefore now no condemnation to those who are in Christ Jesus, who do not walk according to the flesh, but according to the Spirit. For the law of the Spirit of life in Christ Jesus has made me free from the law of sin and death.' - Romans 8:1-2.

'Having now been justified by His blood, we shall be saved from wrath through Him.' - Romans 5:9.

'In Him, we have redemption through His blood, the forgiveness of sins, according to the riches of His grace.' - Ephesians 1:7.

Even though I was a believer and follower of Jesus, I had not yet surrendered and repented of this sin in my life. I was in disobedience. Yet He loved me and gave me much grace. I had to deal with this sin in my life and be free from its power and influence over me. So, I went up to the prayer line at the front of my church one night at the behest of a close friend (to whom I later married!). But something powerful happened at that moment when I received prayer and repented. I felt for the first time that something in my life had been severed and there was a sense that I had broken out of a cycle and pattern that I had been struggling with for years. "Whether it was sexual lust, just pure weakness, couldn't say no, no resistance to temptation, demonic rights and holds and influence over me; whatever it was, I recognised I was in a holding pattern of sin and I was powerless to break free from its hold until this night. Spiritual power and influence were broken then and there, which lifted o my life from that moment on. I was at that place where I could deal with the issue and truly wanted to repent (get right with Father) and be free to move on and do life His way.

5. Confidence

Let me first say that no one is born with self-confidence. I will also add that even though not all intrinsic abilities come from your dad, dads profoundly and significantly influence our lives. Confidence is only one aspect of our lives that is shaped by various factors and dads'.

My mother was always there for me, and I will always appreciate her for that. That said, and I respectfully say this, she could only fill the shoes and roll of 'mother' and not the role of both parents. When a father leaves the home, he leaves his kids and his spouse/partner; both can feel abandoned, betrayed and a host of other things too.

I realise dads are just as prone to sin and to make mistakes and poor calls from time to time as much as the next person, so I am careful not to ascribe to them as being the perfect model upon which I base my whole life. The impact of having a dad in your life is vast, as well as the impact of not having one. But dads instill a sense of strength and confidence into a child, which is carried through into manhood or womanhood.

My point is simply that if/when fathers do leave the family home, they leave a massive void. And even though mine left when I was quite young, the ripple effect began earlier, and some of those ripples can be seen today. But God had a unique and creative way of using those ripples in my life to generate energy that I can use for my life, others and His purposes. I guess the older I got and the more experiences I went through, I became more confident in myself and more assertive in my day-to-day. God has placed people in my life who have helped me come out of my shell, given me space to grow, and become more of the person through experiences, trials and challenging times God always intended me to be. I often found the people who I worked with over the years often rubbed off on me, some good traits and some negative traits. But I have learnt to glean the good, ditch the bad, and hone those things over time.

During my life I have been in many situations where it was a 'crunch time' for me regarding faith and character. It was one day at work quite some years ago, a few of the guys in my work section decided to look at some dirty magazines. They all knew I was a Christian. Then the loudest of them shouted at me, 'Hey Breno, come over here and have a look!', 'It might do you some good.' I yelled back, 'No, I'm right.' They came back with, 'C'mon, be a man!'. I said, 'I already am!' I felt bold and confident that day, allowing me to be a real witness to God and show them that my faith in Him was genuine. A sense of satisfaction and a thought of 'I have grown' came over me. Father God and I, I'm sure, were both pleased. This occasion strengthened me. I also remember that many of the guys who worked there would come up to me privately and ask me to pray for them or their family members for different reasons because I had genuine faith in God. However, the more I stood my ground, the more they seemed to respect me and what I believed in. I had many God appointments to share with them.

As I have grown, I have become more assertive, bold, confident, and determined in what I do and how I do things. Even when there are moments where speaking out is the right thing to do or sticking up for your mates and having their backs. Even the seemingly simple things, such as learning to say 'Yes' when necessary and to say 'No' when necessary and sticking to your guns.

I have been on a personal mission to have my words and actions line up even when I don't feel like it. I strive to be a man of mettle. Subconsciously I want to be the man God intended me to be. Like you, I am a work in progress, and we are making progress.

6. Fear of Others' Opinions & Words

This has been one of the hardest personal issues for me to conquer, fear of others' thoughts and words. What will they think or say about me?

I remember as a teenager when I started learning German/Deutsche from home; I had all my course materials on the dining table, and I enjoyed my learning and progress. One of my uncles, staying with us then, came into the kitchen area where I was studying, started to say some things about the language, and asked me why I was doing this. If I recall correctly, I was so embarrassed and discouraged by his words and how they came across that I sent all the course materials back after that occasion. It was that day that I stopped my learning.

Another example was when I was younger; I was so shy and embarrassed about carrying my Bible. I didn't want anyone to see me with a Bible, let alone what they might say to me or about me. And this was in church as well!

I have been blessed that the Lord has been so gracious to me and placed many good people in my life to help me grow. As time progressed, I started to recognise a formation and solidification of fear (of others) and shame about myself. Not only did I fear other people (their expressions/reactions/opinions/words/thoughts – what I assumed they were thinking), I began to see myself in a way that fell well below how the Lord saw me. My self-confidence was low; my self-estimation was terrible at best; I guess I also felt embarrassed about myself and how I was, and I did not like myself because I felt so inferior and below others. But more on this in the next 'struggle point.' But to finish this line of thought, fear absolutely stifled and greatly limited what I did in life and lowered the level of achievement and success I had.

The work of the Holy Spirit is profound and personal; one course of action doesn't suit all. So how He works with you will be different from my story. But we all share a common goal, to be more Christ-like. Thanks to God, we remain ourselves but are a better version of ourselves. The scales of fear, shame, guilt, embarrassment, and every other weight fall off us over time, sometimes quickly and other times longer.

This may depend on what it is you are dealing with. Whichever the case is for you, God is at work, so keep allowing Him to fulfill His will and purposes in you. Think about this; how will some people come to know Jesus or see God in you if you are not changed and are a witness for Him to others? It's not a guilt trip but an encouragement that you are not the same person now as when the Lord first came into your life when you received Him. As God has blessed you, He has given you gifts and abilities to be a blessing, witness, and example to others.

7. Faulty Thinking

To think faulty is to live faultily. This is a big deal because it affects your whole being, quality of life, and relationships (all of them). And not to mention how you perceive life. My inner thoughts were not an accurate or true description of what the greater reality was presenting. We can ask ourselves, 'What are they thinking?'. But what are they thinking? Sometimes we will never know. What's important is understanding what and who we are to Father God and why Jesus did what He did for us.

On one particular occasion, when I was speaking at my church, I looked around at the congregation, and all I saw were seemingly uninterested and disagreeing faces, angry even. I began to think that the words I was saying were wrong; I felt discouraged, and I also had a sense of embarrassment and shame. I felt exposed. People were seeing through me. These were the thoughts and emotions I was having at that moment. I felt extremely uncomfortable.

But here's the turnaround. At the end of the service, where people were milling around having a chat, I had several people come up to me and say how much they not only liked the message but got many good points from it and wanted to hear me speak again. What?! I could not understand what had just happened.

But later, I realised how powerful that lesson was for me. The Lord was showing me and bringing about change in me, change that has stepped me up and bolstered truth and healing that has progressed me forward in my journey to this point.

Perception does not always accurately depict reality.

What matters most is knowing and understanding what the Word and Spirit of God say about you. Despite our sins and shortcomings, God loves us unconditionally. When you get caught up in your thoughts, they are sometimes less than what others think but incredibly less than what God thinks about us.

For example, I'm a bad person, they don't like me, I'm useless, I can't do it, I'm not smart enough, I'm not funny or good enough, I'm too fat, I'm too skinny, I don't like myself, I'll never achieve anything or go anywhere, no one loves or cares about me, no one would miss me if I die, I am who they say I am, I'm no one special, no one likes me, God likes others more than me, God doesn't want to bless me, I can't lose this weight, I'm not funny or interesting, I'll never get a girl/man, I won't get that job, I'm a failure, I'm beyond help, I'll never change, I'm a loser, it's too late for me know.

I have to stop here! The list is just too large, negative, destructive and untrue for me to continue. These are just some of the common ones we tell ourselves or that we've heard others say about themselves. Unfortunately, this is the world we live in. But this is not the end of the story, far from it.

When I was younger, I read those short stories, Twist a Plot, or Choose Your Own Adventure books. These were great books because the end was not fixed like in a traditional novel or movie you watch. You had a say in your ending or adventure. Your future was open to other options and finales, some good, others not so good. But God has a plan especially for you, different from what you first thought or believed. Did you know that God has already written down all the days of your life in a book?

'You saw me before I was born. Every day of my life was recorded in Your book. Every moment was laid out before a single day had passed.' - Psalm 139:16.

The book of Ephesians says that God from long ago wanted you to do all the good things He specifically made you to accomplish. His plans for you are good and plentiful. There is only one source of truth in our existence: the Lord Himself. He is **THE WAY** and **THE TRUTH** and **THE LIFE!**

Ultimately, your life is not over until God says so. You are not useless, worthless, hopeless, or anything less than what God thinks and says you are. The Bible says we have the mind of Christ and that the renewing of our mind transforms us. Through the power of God's word and Holy Spirit, you and I can be made into a new creation, a brand-new person, and live in the truth that only he can give us.

You see, God is Spirit. He connects with our spirit and begins to do ongoing work via the Holy Spirit that directly affects what we think and how we think and changes our attitudes, behaviours, and perception of the world. Our motives and agendas change, and our interactions with others begin to take on a different expression. Our words and the things we say change. Our direction in life begins to take on a new course. God even plants new desires and plans in our hearts. Life begins to take on new purpose and meaning. There will be a growing sense of belonging, satisfaction, fulfillment and significance in your life. Life will not always be rosy and without problems or difficult times; however, life will never be the same, as now you have the Lord on your side directing, guiding and enabling you through those challenging occasions, as well as the good times.

A Devil and maybe even other people in your circles of life may remind you of your past from time to time, but God is interested in your future. As far as He is concerned, He can use your past experiences to help you and others in their present to help fulfill His plans for their future and yours.

'He comforts us in all our troubles so that we can comfort others. When they are troubled, we will be able to give them the same comfort God has given us.' - 2 Corinthians 1:4.

8. Character

This is another big one for me. I have been working on this one for as long as I can remember. But it is more than just our words lining up with our actions. I have had to work on other character development and integrity aspects intentionally – such things as trustworthiness, ethics, principles, respect and values.

Do you struggle with consistency? What I mean is, do your words and actions line up? I'm talking about integrity. Also, is your personal/private life consistent with your public life? The only person who did this, hands down, was Jesus. He was perfect and sinless. You might think well, that's ok for Him;

he was God, and he doesn't do anything wrong, sinful, evil, immoral, or half-hearted. How can there be a fair comparison? But wait! The difference between Jesus and us is that the Holy Spirit didn't have to work <u>on</u> Jesus to perfect or complete Him in the way He does with us; all the Holy Spirit had to do was work <u>through</u> Jesus. We are a work in progress, and there is much more the Holy Spirit must do in each of us to complete His mission. So, you might be thinking, 'Are we all so broken and damaged?' Well, to an extent, yes. This highlights how much we need the Saviour and the Holy Spirit; to save us from our sins and to save us from ourselves.

The Bible says we are to be more Christ-like. Does he expect us to be perfect in every way? How can I live up to those expectations? I am a flawed human being; how could I rise to a standard that Father God completely understands that we are mere mortals, flawed, imperfect, prone to sin, not whole, incomplete and subject to the effects and influences of a fallen world and any other godless influence or impact? And this is why we need God in our life all the time. The Helper, the Holy Spirit, has been sent to us by Jesus to counsel, guide, help, inspire, correct, convict, empower, enable, direct us and many other things so we can be successful, productive and effective in our life.

The voids and emptiness in our life can only be filled with the power and presence of the Holy Spirit. Those areas where we have lack and weakness can only be truly filled and strengthened by His power. Over the years, I have had many good men of God come and go in my life that, which has instilled into me solid lessons and character-forging moments. Since I lacked a role model, God put into my life men of concrete character and tested faith to help shape and bolster my faith and convictions; it 'just happened' that people would be in my life at the right time to confront me, discipline me, and direct and encourage me to get my life on track that would lay a course that would lead me to success and not to failure.

As men, we need other strong men in our lives to get our attention and guide us on the proper road. We can lose our sense of direction very easily and quickly. We can even convince ourselves that we don't need the help and are okay. But denial is deadly, mainly if your life depends on it when you are not meeting your issues or problems head-on.

When you deny yourself, you deny the one who wants to deliver you.

Think about this: If you were stronger than your problems, then why do you still struggle with them? How is it that you are constantly caught up in your pattern of sin? If you are ok and don't need help, why do you seek change but never seem to attain it? Why are you still struggling to find a way out of your situation? Why do you still hurt? How do you cope with the harm, lack or loss from your past?

Who do you have in your life to help you out with your situation?

Call them now and seek their help. We are not promised tomorrow, so make the most of your time today.

If you find that no one comes to mind, I will encourage you to seek the support/advice of a trusted stranger. What I mean by this is someone who has a long and reliable reputation that the people around them say good and trustworthy things. You may know of their work or ministry, and they are within your reach to contact them. I would tell you to surround yourself with good company and help people if this is for you. Surround yourself now with new people. Perhaps you need to let go and get away from certain people currently in your life that no longer need to be there.

To get new results, we must take new measures.

Your situation is unique, and your next move will also be. If you can speak to someone, you can trust and seek guidance before you make significant decisions; this is also a good thing. If you are in a position where you can speak to someone you trust, it's now time to begin taking charge of yourself. Share a problem, pray about it, make practical steps to resolve and make progress. This may be with your home group leader, youth pastor, or best friend, who can give you some good advice. Be intentional about taking steps to your next breakthrough, your next step on your personal journey. Be encouraged and stay the course. You're not alone and not the only one going through what you are dealing with. Others have travelled the road that you are now on. Take and learn from them their experience and advice that helped see them through.

Here are a few points to consider:

A. Get connected / Stay connected
B. Be accountable / Open to trusted people
C. Be determined / Persevere / Be Tenacious
D. Pray a lot / Listen a lot / Learn what you can
E. Write things down so you won't forget
F. Be encouraged / Encourage others

If there is anything above you can relate to or identify with, I want you to remember these **Points of Struggle** for later on because as you progress through your process, you will see a stark difference in your life and how you see yourself. You will be encouraged, and always consider making time to thank God. This is your time to transform.

CHAPTER 2: TYPES OF DADS

There are many kinds of dads out there, but I will only focus on four types here. These 'dad types' are of my personal position, so I will not claim they are based on professional premises.

You may see your dad in one of these examples or have a different dad type or maybe even a mixture of more than one 'type.'

Avoidance Dad

Not around much or at all. Does not want to be involved or be part of your life. Acting out of fear and not taking responsibility. Lack of strength and character. Not being an example. Overwhelmed or under too much pressure. Did not want to fail or make mistakes. Not supportive.

Absent Dad

Died or left before you were born/or at a very young age. Prison. Deployed. Emotionally detached. Was in the house but not in your life. Was around but not overly involved with you on a regular basis. Too busy or interested in other things. Not supporting you at your most needed times. Rarely made it to a graduation, other noteworthy and important events, and other social or sporting occasions.

Abusive Dad

Physical. Violent. Emotional. Verbal. Addiction or trauma issues. Sexual. Harmful.

Abundant Dad

Not perfect, but present. Available. Helpful. Shared life experiences and knowledge. Showed love. Modeled being a dad.

Which of these 'dads' fits your experience?

Can you relate to any of these?

How did this type of dad shape your life or define your path?

What were your responses to his choices and actions?

Take some time out to think.

But asking yourself some further questions will show you where you are, how you will respond, and what you are willing to do to move forward.

Where exactly are you at in life? Are you at a place where you want to do something about what is happening within you? Are you clear-minded or unclear about what happened? What are your attitudes, thoughts and emotions toward your dad?

Is it possible here that there is absolutely no chance that you will ever consider or want even to heal and restore a relationship with your dad?

Maybe you don't want a relationship with him or even want to meet or get to know him, but it's more about your own peace that you want to do something. No one is saying you have to have a relationship with your dad, but God can help you change the things within you.

Tough questions require honest answers. I can understand that it's not easy or natural to do what would go against the grain of your soul, but I know from personal change that I am better off for it. This could be your time to get the wheels in motion which will help transition you from questions to statements. So, this could mean for you something like going from: **'Can I forgive him?'** to **'I can forgive him.'** This statement may seem quite unlikely to you right now, but it is attainable if you are willing and determined. It is not up to him; it is up to you. You see, forgiveness will set <u>you</u> free. It is one of the most liberating and freeing things you will ever do.

Forgiveness is for you, and for him. When you can think of that person who is your biological father and no longer have any anger, anxiety, fear, hate, unforgiveness, resentment, stress or any other symptom, then you could probably say that you have come to that place where you have peace within yourself, and towards him as well. You may not love him or like what he did or didn't do, but all those awful things that affected you up to this point will no longer have the sting or power on or over your life any further. These are the things you want to get rid of from your life.

I would think then that if you are reading this book, you are at a place where you want to make and see changes happen. Good for you! If I can, I would like to tell you how I worked things out so that it provides a roadmap and offers suggestions for you to make your move.

CHAPTER 3: MY PROCESS

Climbing the high road takes you to the top of the mountain. It is not the easier path to take, but the victory is greater. In my journey, I had to overcome four major issues.

1. **My Justification**
2. **My Will and Emotions**
3. **My Commitment**
4. **My Thoughts and Words**

My Justification

'I suffered from his choices.'

'My life changed because of his actions.'

'I have gone through hardship and been a casualty due to that selfish individual.'

'I have a right to be angry, resentful, and have negative and hateful thoughts about him. He did this to me.'

Those are all pretty strong words; though not all of these represent my once-held position, they are terms that many hold as justification to think, feel and live as they do. Do you justify your position? For you could say and hold to these things and deem these things as reasonable considering your past events. But to live righteously and freely, we must look at things from an entirely different perspective and understand that we will progress.

At the start of history, humanity did something wrong to God in the first place; no human being has any right to hold on to the past; only God, but He had other plans. Even though He would have been fully justified in Himself not to forgive humanity, He graciously did.

Consider the following six points.

1. Love: 'For God loved the world (YOU) so much that He gave His one and only Son so that everyone who believes in Him will not perish but have eternal life.' - John 3:16.

It's pretty clear why God would do such a powerful thing as this. The love of Jesus held him to that cross for you and me. That weapon of torture was, at the same time, a symbol of love and hope for every person. When we think about the cross Jesus hung on, we see love, no conditions, no strings. It's just a matter of repentance and putting our faith and trust in Him. God has always loved you and always will love you.

Do we deserve this? No way. But He does anyway. He first loved us. Father God intensely desires a closer relationship with us, and now is the time to get closer to Him and to know Him in a more real, closer, profound, and personal way. He is waiting for you to come to Him so you can get to know Him better. He will never abandon you, leave you, ditch you, disown you, or quit on you. He doesn't look at you and wait for you to make mistakes; he's so wrapped around you He can't take His eyes off you. He actually thinks about you a lot.

'How precious are Your thoughts about me, O God, they cannot be numbered!' - Psalms 139:17.

2. Goodness: '...The goodness (kindness/graciousness) of God leads you to repentance.' - Romans 2:4.

The Lord cannot deny Himself, His character, His word or His nature. This means, He is unchangeable; he cannot help but express who He is and how He does things, particularly when we don't deserve His forgiveness or anything good from Him. The essence and substance of God show us how catastrophic sin is and how it separates us from Him completely. Sin destroys us and prevents us from knowing Him personally. The consequences of sin form an 'uncrossable' gap between Him and us. Though sin separates us from the love of God, **'...nothing can ever separate us from God's love'**. - Romans 8:38. The difference between God and us is that He can exist without us, not the other way round; we can't exist without Him.

God the Father, without deservingness from us, has provided us with a way out of all our troubles, situations, sins, scars, tears and fears. His name is Jesus. Everything awful, bad, sinful and godless in us put Him on that rugged cross, and it came at the highest cost, Himself. Everything that is good, loving, kind, gracious, generous and wonderful comes from Him, and He gives these gifts to us. As human beings, we are not in a position to call the shots to Him, do the things we are inclined to do or hold on to the things we think are ok or acceptable. Not everything in life is good for us. He is all-powerful and all-knowing; we are just mere mortals, highly treasured. But as we yield to Him and trust Him, we get everything He has to offer for nothing. It's the best deal we will ever get. **We give Him our worst in return for His best.**

3. Faithfulness: 'God will make this happen, for He who calls you is faithful.' - 1 Thessalonians 5:24.

God has your back. When God makes a promise to you, He does not break it. He cannot undo what He says. He is against His unchangeable nature to go against His life-giving word. He is both a promise maker and a promise keeper. When He speaks to you personally, He says, **'You can trust Me; this is a sure thing I am saying to you; I will show you that you can have confidence in Me.'**

Let me throw a question: What emotions do you feel when it comes to your dad and God? How do you feel about your dad? How do you feel about God? Do you see them as totally different, or do you relate to them similarly?

At this point, I would like to suggest an activity that might help you look at your feelings/emotions with clarity. The first thing to do is list your emotions and feelings about your dad. Then, make a second list to help you identify your feelings/emotions towards God. Then we will compare the two lists.

An interesting point is **how you see and relate to your dad is often reflective of how you see and relate to God.** In the second part of this book, I will share how God has been and is a Father to me. And how He can be a Father to you too.

While writing your lists or completing them, you may need to take some time out for yourself, cool off, or take some slow, deep breaths. Please do. Take your time with this. Come back when you're ready because things may rise to the surface in you if they haven't started already. There could be negative thoughts, intense emotions, or memories. When the past rises to the surface in your heart and soul, the Holy Spirit can more easily handle that and soothe, mend, renew, restore, encourage and strengthen you. To move forward, allow the Holy Spirit as much time as He needs to do His healing and counseling work. He is the best at doing this for you. He knows how to handle you. This is an important time and step for you. Please ensure you are in a quiet place with no interruptions, noise, disturbances, or anything else that will interfere with your time. **'When you pray, go into your room, and when you have shut your door, pray to your Father who is in the secret place, and your Father who sees in secret will reward you openly.'** - Matthew 6:6. He is waiting for you. Consider praying the following before you begin writing. And wait for Him to respond.

'Holy Spirit, I need your help as I start this healing process. I cannot do this on my own. I give you full permission to come into my heart and soul to begin your work. Please take from me all the heartache, the hurt, the pain, the torment, the negative emotions, and the painful memories. I ask you to heal me and change my heart and soul to be how you intended me to be. Please speak to me now and guide me gently, healingly. Help me forgive, and show me how to let go of anything you see in me as harmful or hindering. Father, show yourself strong and faithful in my life now, especially this time. Change my heart and help me to find ways to change any attitude that is detrimental to my relationship with you and others. Please help me to be willing to change even when I don't feel like it. Please show me your presence, power, and provision at this time. In Jesus' name, Amen.'

> Ok, if you are now ready, let's begin. First, write down the 'Dad' list. Then, cover that list with paper and write down the 'God' list. After you have done that, compare the two lists. Interestingly, it turned out that several points on my two lists where I struggled with my dad were the very things I struggled with God also. You might find this for yourself too. The lists you have written are your own personal lists showing you where you are in your life right now. This is your story and how it relates to you.

Now it's your turn.

A. Your emotions/feelings towards/about your dad

B. Your emotions/feelings towards/about Father God

PART 1: DADLESS...

LIST A   **LIST B**

Okay, now that you have your lists, it is time to start looking at and working through your points. One point at a time is excellent; pace yourself as you move forward with matters of the heart. Some issues will take longer than others to work through. None of these is a quick fix. As time, learning and healing go on; you will find that your comparative lists will change for the better. You will also find that how you relate to each will vary. This is an indication of your progress.

With the above prayer that you went through, that was to get you into a place to position you for progress and to allow the Holy Spirit time and opportunity to move in your life and to speak to you personally. Only by His ability and love for you can get to this place and move on from there with real results.

A quick prayer...

'Father God, I don't know how You will do it, but help me to trust in You to make changes in my life and situation. I choose to put my faith and trust in You so You can come in and work Your power directly in my life now. Make me a new person with a new future, a new heart, and a new start. In Your powerful name Jesus.'

At this point, I would encourage you to take some time out and let Him take over. No distractions, quietly being with Him. Allow Him to move in your life and speak to you. He is waiting for you. Here are a few practical and encouraging verses.

'The end of a thing is better than its beginning.' - Ecclesiastes 7:8.

'Do not hasten in your spirit to be angry.' - Ecclesiastes 7:9.

'Do not be hasty to go from His presence.' - Ecclesiastes 8:3. (This verse has a different context, but the words are good advice to stay with the Lord for longer, it is worth it!)

'When I thought to understand this, (Regarding what you have gone through and why) **it was too painful for me until I went into the sanctuary** (presence) **of God; Then I understood...'** - Psalm 73:16-17. (He brings us understanding, healing and closure/resolve when we include Him in the process.)

I want to do something else practical with you now. This will help you work through your journey of transformation. The following is a list of words that help define what you might be grappling with. I have included these as guides to help you pray through. They can help you clarify and understand what you're feeling, thinking, and dealing with. Jesus said: **'Take My yoke upon you. Let Me teach you because I am gentle and humble at heart, and you will find rest for your souls.'** - Matthew 11:29.

The goal here is to read through each word, circle Yes or No, and pray through the words that relate to you. These words could mean what you have gone through or how you interact with others due to your experiences. Ask the Lord to show you the root cause and to break off the effects and impacts of these harmful/hurtful connections. There is a lot here, so give it some time. We must be specific in dealing with particular issues to get definite results. Also, write down any other word/s that affect you. To track your personal growth and change, you could revisit this list after six or twelve months and be encouraged by your progress.

Have you ever been or felt...

Abandoned - YES / NO

Abused - YES / NO

Afraid - YES / NO

Angry - YES / NO

Anxious - YES / NO

Arrogant - YES / NO

Betrayed - YES / NO

Bitter - YES / NO

Broken - YES / NO

Damaged - YES / NO

Depressed - YES / NO

Despised - YES / NO

Disappointed - YES / NO

Discouraged/Discouraging - YES / NO

Disrespectful - YES / NO

Fearful - YES / NO

Hateful - YES / NO

Hopeless - YES / NO

Hot tempered - YES / NO

Impatient - YES / NO

Inconsiderate - YES / NO

Insecure - YES / NO

Intolerant - YES / NO

Lost - YES / NO

Rejected - YES / NO

Resentful - YES / NO

Stressed - YES / NO

Tormented/Tormentful - YES / NO

Unforgiving - YES / NO

Weak - YES / NO

Worthless - YES / NO

I realise these words are a lot to tackle, but you don't need to take all of them on right now. Remember, it is a process. The restoration takes time. It's in your timeframe, so take as much as you can handle. Several of the above emotions are not necessarily bad in themselves. Still, past events may be causing some of these to be having an unhealthy/damaging or amplified effect on you and others.

Let me explain one's journey in these terms; A map is only good for reference if you know where you are and where you are headed. So, if you have been praying and working through any of the above points, it's like you have been on one side of a riverbank for a considerable length of your life, but it is now time to make your way to the other.

Your situation may be that you wanted to move on, but there was no means to get to the riverbank on the opposite side. Well, this is your time to know that Jesus, your boat, is before you and ready to take you to that point, and from there, you both journey on together. I might add that if you are not in a place to confront certain issues, that's ok. Timing is crucial to your personal, emotional, spiritual and psychological health. It is also Father's desire and will to come alongside you and walk you through your personal journey.

The following words are His heart for you: **'He lets me rest in green meadows; He leads me beside peaceful streams. He renews my strength. He guides me along right paths.'** - Psalm 23:2-3. Open, green pastures and streams speak of a place of safety and soothing. It also says being in the right place for your peace and best interest.

You could also go through the following activity to help target other areas you might be contending with. If you look at the following list, you may see points as to where you are right now leading to where you want to be. Ask Father God to help you move forward from one side to the other side as you go

PART 1: DADLESS...

through your list. Mark or highlight each point that applies to you, declare out loud, and know that God is listening to you and working on your behalf.

You may also find it insightful to speak with someone who can help you through those tough points. I also find dating events in your life important for reference and encouraging reminders as to when God moved in your life or on your behalf.

Father, in Jesus' name, take me from that place of feeling or being...

Abused to **Healed / Whole / Loved and Respected!**
Afraid to **Bold / Brave and Courageous!**
Angry to **Peaceful / Settled!**
Anxious to be **At Ease / Calm / Relaxed!**
Arrogance to **Humble and Respectful!**
Bitter to **Content and Welcoming!**
Broken to **Whole and Complete!**
Damaged to **Healed and Healthy!**
Depressed to **Joyous / Strong and Hearty!**
Despising to be **Positive / Open!**
Disappointed to **Satisfied / Content!**
Discouraged to **Encouraged!**
Disrespectful to **Respectful!**
Fearful to **Confident / Composed!**
Hating to **Loving / Kind!**
Hopeless to **Hopeful / Assured!**
Hot Tempered to **Self-Controlled / Calm!**

Impatient to **Patient / Contentment!**

Inconsiderate to **Considerate /Kind!**

Insecure to **Confident / Certain!**

Intolerant to **Tolerant / Understanding!**

Lost to **Placed / Positioned / Purposed!**

Rejected to **Accepted / Sense of Belonging!**

Resentment to **Showing Goodwill!**

Stressed to **Restful / Relaxed!**

Tormented to **Serene / Soothed!**

Unforgiving to **Forgiving / Pardoning!**

Weak to **Strong / Determined / Principled!**

Worthless to **Worthy / Valuable / Valued / Useful / Treasured!**

I trust at this point; you are experiencing the power and presence of God in your life. It would help if you had a miracle and breakthrough, and now is the time. To get the changes we seek, breakthroughs, and fruitfulness in our life, it is important to, as often as we can, maintain a position and a response of faith with thanksgiving. This shift your focus and placement of where you are looking onto the one (Father) who alone can make things happen. This makes all the difference, especially with sensitive and complex issues. The life Father God wants us to live is filled with victory, absolute joy and breakthroughs.

Now, not to come across as negative, but at times, it is very easy/tempting to slip back into the 'old/normal' way of thinking. It can also happen quickly to slip back into the old and normal way of speaking and behaving too. Changing how we think and our thoughts' content brings about change and transformation.

Also, our attitude determines our behaviour. **Our mental pacts determine our physical acts.**

'Be transformed by the renewing of your mind.' - Romans 12:2. **We must speak the change to see the change.**

'Let us hold fast the confession of our hope without wavering, for He who promised is faithful.' - Hebrews 10:23. Father God is at work and will finish what He started. **'And I am certain that God, who began the good work within you, will continue His work until it is finally finished on the day when Christ Jesus returns.'** - Philippians 1:6.

For broken hearts and broken spirits, the Lord promises that **'...I will give you a new heart, and I will put a new spirit in you.'** - Ezekiel 36:26.

Later in this book, there will be more about Will and Emotions, Thoughts, and Words.

If you are experiencing some out-of-the-ordinary feelings, thoughts, or seemingly left-field circumstances, take courage and know that you are on the right track. You are headed in the right direction.

Something else to consider here: Different types of beings wants to cause you harm, danger, and derailment. Let me explain. God is spirit, and He created the angels. Most angels chose to stay with Him, and the rest chose to check out and go their own wild way.

We know them as demons, and it would seem that the Devil, Satan, would be the ringleader of these fallen/evil angels. These 'beings' absolutely hate you and me simply because we are made in God's image, loved by God, and have the privilege of getting into the right relationship with Him. This is only possible through believing in and receiving His one and only son, Jesus.

I point out that we are in the crosshairs of this spiritual enemy, with spiritual and physical outworking's and outcomes. Not everything we experience is a random event or coincidence. When you have a glimpse of the big picture, through God's word, you can begin to start connecting the dots. You and I and every other believer and follower of Jesus are on the hit list from hell.

We must become aware, identify and recognise that there is more at work in and upon our lives. I will go through this in more detail later in this book. But this is relevant to all of us as we all need to understand what is going on as we move closer to the Lord and receive what He has for us. It will help us to realise what is really going on. There is more at work here, and this other reality needs to be called out. Therefore, it is important to know and declare the word of God to extinguish all those fiery arrows the enemy shoots at us. For example, we start to get our life in order, and things start to go sideways. This could be with relationships, business, confusion, circumstances, or situations going haywire; not always, but things seem to be going crazy all of a sudden. These things are not so random, but more on these later.

4. Gentleness: 'Come to Me, all of you who are weary and carry heavy burdens, and I will give you rest.' - Matthew 11:28.

'He will not crush the weakest reed or put out a flickering candle.' - Matthew 12:20.

'Go out and stand before Me on the mountain,' the Lord told him. And as Elijah stood there, the Lord passed by, and a mighty windstorm hit the mountain. It was such a terrible blast the rocks were torn loose, but the Lord was not in the wind. After the wind, there was an earthquake, but the Lord was not in the earthquake. And after the earthquake, there was a fire, but the Lord was not in the fire. And after the fire, there was the sound of a gentle whisper.' - 1 Kings 19:11-12.

Father God will never pressure you, though He may prompt, tell or impress on you a word or response; He will never overpower you, manipulate, coerce, tempt, coax, force, or make you do anything against your own free will. He will never impose His will, power, or presence in or upon your life without your voluntary surrender. He cares for you more than you could possibly know or imagine.

He wants the best for you, and He has the best for you - Himself.

Let me ask you something. If there was only one thing that you would want to do with the Lord or have Him do with you, what would that be? As a son to his father or as a daughter to her father, what would that experience look like for you? I think that there is at least one memorable (amongst many others) experience that a son or daughter would want to remember forever having with their dad.

Let me tell you about one of mine.

In heaven, I see myself walking up to Lord Jesus and seeing Him with open arms and a smile on His face waiting to welcome me into His home. Then He puts His arms around me, tells me He's pleased with me, and says, 'I love you, Brendon, welcome home.' He then invites me to go for a walk, and we talk for a while. And just as I take my son's hand and take him for a walk, I would also like Him to do this with me. This would be my eternal present. I sometimes think about this.

We would desire to have all the things in a dad and to experience those things; Father God so desires those things to be in our life. God wants to give what we were never given. So, in this regard, I want to talk about some other relevant points later which will bring home what Father God's heart is all about.

5. Identity: I believe it is essential to ask ourselves at least two fundamental questions: 'Who am I?' and 'Whose am I?' When you become 'born again,' **You belong to the Lord God, the father of Jesus.** You go through a process of becoming a brand-new person, a new creation. **'This means that anyone who belongs to Christ has become a new person. The old life is gone; a new life has begun.'** - 2 Corinthians 5:17.

You came into this world with certain physical features because you took on the DNA and genes your parents passed on to you. When you look at yourself in the mirror, you can see similarities and likenesses to them. A good friend I haven't seen in years surprised me with how much more he looks like his dad the older he gets. It also holds that the longer you have a relationship with Father God, the more you are with Him, and the more you will begin to 'look' and be more just like Him. People will see God in you.

'Then God said, 'Let us make man in our image, to be like us.' - Genesis 1:26.

It would be best if you were encouraged to know that **you were made on purpose for a purpose.** And while God did not intend for you to go through all those difficult years and times, God also wants to work in you and through you for His greater good. While some fathers have the title of 'Dad,' they don't necessarily hold that responsibility. Father God, on the other hand, holds both. Life has relevance, significance, meaning, and purpose when we understand how we came into being and why. In the second part of this book, I will share how God is a father - to me. But also, how He desires to be a father to you.

The basis for our identity (in contrast to our natural parents) should also come from the fact that God is our creator, we are His creation, and He has a creative purpose for us. Our identity should not come from what we do, how we live, how well off we are, or how much knowledge we have. Our true identity is found only in Jesus. We are made in His likeness; we were intricately and skillfully made; we are a new creation in Him; we have explanations and reasons for being in Him. **When you take God out of the equation of life, then life is no equation.** There is no real purpose, means, intention, value, benefit, end game or grounds for any logic or reason for being here. Existence, then, would just be a meaningless and senseless event.

If God were non-existent, there would be no absolutes; everything would be subjective, so who can say what is right or wrong? What is moral, and what is deemed immoral? Who would have the right or authority to set a standard or benchmark to say what is evil and good? If these standards come from a human being, then these things are biased and flawed at best. The only perfect and valid basis for morality, justice, fairness, and identity comes from a powerful, all-knowing, excellent, absolute source.

If we base our existence, who we are, and our reason for life on anything other than Father God, we will always have a flawed, imperfect, distorted and incomplete view of who we really are. You are either a son or daughter of God. As you begin to understand, put together and recognise the truth of this matter, all the pieces of the plan fit together perfectly. It makes reasonable sense and is logical.

Belonging is another aspect of identity. Every human being has an innate desire or need to be needed, wanted and to be part of something more than themselves. We all want to be accepted. The good thing about God is that He wants us, and we have a strong sense of belonging, identity and purpose with Him. But what about your social circles? Who do you associate with? Which club, organisation, or membership do you associate with? Who do you hang out with? Why are you in those circles? How does it make you feel to be part of that group? Why are you there? You will, of course, have varying answers to these questions.

The bottom line is we want to bond and belong with others. It's one of our deepest longings. We all were made with God's imprinted likeness to relate, love, connect, and coexist.

Self-worth is yet another facet of identity. It's effortless to compare ourselves with others, especially those who, from our perspective, are recognised and appreciated, or others ask and value their opinions over yours. **The difference is that you may be their last resort to them, but to God, you are His first choice**.

While others may not have you high on their list, we don't hold everyone we know high on our list either. We have our own 'order' of people around us. This is natural. Your opinion of yourself is not always a true reflection of reality. You will never see the truth about yourself if you continue looking at yourself through a 'carnival mirror' — distorted at best. This is why we need the Father's perspective and His Spirit of truth to show us who we really are and what we mean to Him.

Here are some encouraging Scriptures.

'And Your thoughts toward us cannot be recounted to You in order; If I would declare and speak of them, they are more than can be numbered.' - Psalms 40:5.

'For I know the plans and thoughts that I have for you says the Lord, plans for peace and well-being and not for disaster, to give you a future and a hope.' - Jeremiah 29:11.

'For we (you) are His workmanship (His own masterwork, a work of art), created in Christ Jesus (reborn from above — spiritually transformed, renewed, ready to be used) for good works, which God prepared (for us) beforehand (taking paths which He set) so that we would walk in them (living the good life which He prearranged and made ready for us).' - Ephesians 2:10.

When we look at our natural fathers (through the lens of life) to try and get an idea of our identity, sense of belonging, self-worth, or value, we will always have a distorted and flawed picture. We take on the likenesses of our physical father, and we inherit features, traits, attitudes and sometimes behaviours just like theirs, or similar ones at any rate. Though you are individual and unique, you can't deny or evade what has been passed to you. And from him, you are the next generation. We may not have the ability, power or say to control what happened to us in our past. Still, we have more power, control, voice, ability and capacity over our present and future circumstances.

6. Rights: You have every right to feel...(whatever you feel). But, do you have the right to remain...(how do you feel)? This a fair and reasonable question. Especially those feelings we 'rightly justify' because of what others have done to us during our life.

In terms of physical and psychological ability or wellbeing, whatever emotional state we are in, it is impossible to remain in that state of emotion forever. We also ought not to stay in one emotional state for long. For various reasons, it's not human, sustainable, or healthy. Whether it is a physical or mental issue, your mind and body cannot sustain any one emotional state all the time. Either your body will start to feel the effects, or your mind/mental well-being can also be affected.

We each have our limitations, as do our body's natural defense mechanisms. You and I are emotional beings that must get things out/express ourselves. Albeit emotional expression can either heal or hinder us, like grieving. One cannot put a timeframe or formula for dealing with grief. Grieving helps us deal with loss and confront the hurt and pain, but if we cannot continue to live life with support or purpose (not to forget or deny the cause or reason), this can become an unhealthy way of living.

Opening up and releasing emotions helps us manage and move ahead, which can aid us in improving our lives. I Remember a conversation with my uncle, who lost his wife and son. He told me at his wife's funeral that he wasn't even over his son's passing. I asked him how he coped. He responded, 'I don't cope; I manage it.' This, sadly, is many people's experience. I would say here that people, more often than not, go through life doing the hard yards in their strength. Father God understands loss and is well-equipped to support and soothe you in your loss too.

PART 1: DADLESS...

On another front, in life we will face offense and some form of struggle at some point. Difficult times come and go, and many other life situations can make us feel multiple emotions simultaneously. Emotions are not destructive in themselves; they are simply part of who we are, making us human. The important thing for everyone with Jesus is **His life is our example**. We know that Jesus got angry, He wept, He had joy, He had sorrow, and He suffered - physically and emotionally. He also had spiritual opposition to contend with. But He never let His emotions dictate or control Him. When we observe how the Lord did life here on earth, He was as human and emotional as the rest of us, while at the same time being God. Jesus related to us at every fundamental level. He identified as a human being and experienced life in every way you and I do. Emotions do have their role and place in our life but staying angry at someone, for instance, will only have a detrimental effect on us.

I have been assaulted and insulted several times throughout my life, physically and verbally abused, and discriminated against about my belief in God, my gender, and of course, my race. I have been mocked for having convictions regarding my faith and living a Christ-like lifestyle.; simply by being a Christian. I have often been treated 'differently' and seen as 'weird,' 'weak,' and 'out there due to my faith and in following the Bible is - the word of God. But I assure you, this is the least of my worries as I live following His word. In terms of eternity, these are fleeting experiences to endure and small prices to pay because of what He has done for me, which will last for eternity.

If He can live and die for me, the very least I can do is life and serve Him. When humanity sinned, did God stay angry? Of course, He didn't. Jesus was humanity's saving grace. Also, in

His love for us, He disciplines us. Also, God is the only one that is totally justified in judging us for our sins or holding a grudge, but in His compassion, grace and love, he does not. Though in His holiness and perfect righteousness, He could.

So how can we truly forgive or love others if we have not experienced His love or forgiveness? You might feel justified in holding on to anger, unforgiveness or resentment towards another person, people or group. Still, when Christ is in the equation of life, this is not reasonable or justifiable for us. I'll explain.

No Christ = No Forgiveness Required.

Christ = Forgiveness Required.

Which is true?

Which is right?

Let me clarify.

No Christ = No Forgiveness Required

No Jesus means no God, which means no absolute right or wrong. This would mean that these concepts are merely humanly devised and subjective in every way. Every human being will have their own notion and personal standard of what is right and what is wrong. Or what is good and what is evil. What would be moral, and what would be immoral? There would be no absolute benchmark, level, or line in the sand to show where right/wrong, good/evil and moral/immoral meet or separate. The lines would be biased and blurred at best.

In this framework, if someone somehow hurt you, they might think they have not done ill towards you. Then, as a reaction from you, you might get back at them with revenge or some other harmful response and be fully convinced that your actions were proper, justified, or reasonable.

In this context, forgiveness is a human construct that endeavours to improve or help us feel better about ourselves. Why forgive if there is no ethical, moral or spiritual reason, requirement or basis? You could then legitamise almost any behaviour and call it ok, right, moral, ethical, justified, appropriate or reasonable.

'Even Gentiles, who do not have God's written law, show that they know His law when they instinctively obey it, even without having heard it. They demonstrate that God's law is written in their hearts, for their own conscience and thoughts either accuse them or tell them they are doing right.' - Romans 2:14-15.

From the beginning of human history until now, every individual has had an inbuilt, default understanding of right and wrong. Simply put, a conscience. Why does a child (or anyone for that matter) feel afraid, guilty or ashamed when they do something 'wrong'? And why do they feel good or peaceful when they do something 'right'?

You, I, and every other person that has ever existed or will ever exist had and will have a conscience that simply tells us something is either 'right' or 'wrong,' 'good' or 'evil.' It's like (to oversimplify) our mind, which knows, tells our heart, holds the emotions, and passes a judgment that makes us feel uncomfortable or comfortable about a certain event or course of action. If we're honest, we know when we do or say something right or wrong, good or bad. We don't need anyone to tell us; we intuitively know, right? Think back to any situation you were in, and you may remember when your 'personal internal advisor' spoke to you, affirming or informing you of the morality of that particular situation or course of action. Can anyone really honestly deny such a personal process? Conscience is objective in nature because the perfect and objective God hardwired this within us.

The bottom line is that if there is no Christ, then there is no God-given conscience and no absolute or perfect standard for good/evil, right or wrong, or anything else. This means it's ok to do whatever you want (there will be consequences, of course), but there is no point or purpose in deciding what to do and how you live your life. There is no objective reasoning, responsibility, or obligation. Everything is personal, subjective and flawed.

Switching gears: **Always aim to have a quality of life rather than a high standard of living.** Although nice things are nice, if you continue to hold unforgiveness in your heart and mind, you may miss out on a better life; instead, you will be living a bitter life. Carrying unforgiveness around with you will anchor you, reduce your ability to let go, and you could have a life that will always be short of something that is healthy, whole, fulfilling, favoured and blessed. **"When you avoid forgiveness, you miss out on restoration.**

Is unforgiveness affecting your life?

Christ = Forgiveness Required

Here is a truth: Forgiveness is for you and the other person or party.

This statement may also be extended to the other party and give a sense of reconciliation. My pastor always displayed and taught me that forgiving is one thing. If possible, it is also beneficial to seek reconciliation – a mending of a relationship, a settling of differences, a compromise or coming to an understanding, an end to hostilities, or even having or working towards amiability and peace. I have seen too many good people lose good relationships because of a failure to 'overlook' or get past shallow or superficial issues or misunderstandings. Let's face it; it's too late to leave things undone or not take the initiative to set things straight. Life is too precious to let slip with occasional minor differences. My thought here is that not everything that happens is your fault. But you do have complete control over how you respond to circumstances.

So, when 'stuff' comes your way, you can learn a lesson from the Aikido martial art and be ready to deflect and throw off others' attacks of negativity, harm, thoughtlessness and any other careless or selfish word or act. However, life and processing stuff takes time, and so does learning from experiences, dealing better and more constructively with issues, and handling others in certain situations. You can do this by giving yourself time to settle after a crisis, thinking and seeking others' advice, and praying before confronting the other person or situation. Go into the situation with an attitude that you want a good outcome, but that may not always be the result. Do what you know you need to do and try and move on quickly from that. When you find yourself between 'offense' and 'opportune time,' use that time to get yourself right, or to move into a good/better place, then prayerfully, if that is what you are to do, move forward in trying to address the matter.

Sometimes having someone else with you can be accommodating too, possibly neutral. When you know that you have taken steps to move forward and make things right, you can walk away and know that the burden is not on you. I will also add to this thought that giving thanks to the Lord that He is with you through this and He has given you His grace, means and ability to manage and deal with the situation. I also ask the Lord to help me grow and learn from moments like these, then to be used to help others in the future.

'Work at living in peace with everyone, and work at living a holy life, for those who are not holy will not see the Lord.' - Hebrews 12:14.

'For since our friendship with God was restored by the death of His Son while we were still HIs enemies, we will certainly be saved through the life of His Son.' - Romans 5:10.

'And all of this is a gift from God, who brought us back to Himself through Christ. And God has given us this task of reconciling people to Him. For God was in Christ, reconciling the world to Himself, no longer counting people's sins against them. And He gave us this wonderful message of reconciliation. So we are Christ's ambassadors; God is making His appeal through us. We speak for Christ when we plead, 'Come back to God!' For God made Christ, who never sinned, to be the offering for our sin so that we could be made right with God through Christ.' - 2 Corinthians 5:18-21.

God created human beings, but human beings stepped away from Him, but He loved humankind so much that He made it possible to restore that relationship with Him. And that was through His Son - Jesus, the Saviour, our Saviour.

Now, this may be tough for you because you didn't ask for the hardship you endured, the abuse you experienced, or the upbringing you had; But God, the loving Father, understands what you went through and what you are facing right now. His own Son was treated with physical and verbal violence, and abuse and ridicule. The people around Him tormented him, and He also personally experienced betrayal. He grew up in a humble environment and worked hard His entire life. He was despised and hated just for who He was, who He said He was, and what He did. But He was about His Father's will. God has a plan for you to be whole, well, strong, joyful, purposeful, free, blessed and balanced.

Like yourself, the issues I had to work through came at specific points in my life; some could be dealt with quickly, while other of my life's issues were resolved or worked through over time. You believed and received when you believed in Christ and invited Him into your life. Your spirit immediately became a new creation. The rest of you may have remained the same, your body, mind, will, emotions, etc. But your spirit was transformed instantly!

'This means that anyone who belongs to Christ has become a new creation (person). The old life is gone; a new life has begun!' - 2 Corinthians 5:17.

The work of the Holy Spirit is ongoing.

It is a timely thing that you have begun reading this book. It is no coincidence, either. But instead, there is an appointment to which you have been drawn to set things in order in your own life. This is your time to get issues and matters of the heart and mind worked out and finally dealt with. It is time for you to move on in your life, and Father God wants to use you also to help others who have been through similar situations.

'He comforts us in all our troubles so that we can comfort others. When they are troubled, we will be able to give them the same comfort God has given us.'- 2 Corinthians 1:4.

Father God wants to see you become emotionally, psychologically and spiritually free so you can truly live the way He has always intended for you to be. Here is another truth... **'Stay alert! Watch out for your great enemy, the Devil. He prowls around like a roaring lion, looking for someone to devour.'** - 1 Peter 5:8.

And...

'Stand firm against him, and be strong in your faith.' - 1 Peter 5:9.

We must be aware of our common enemy, stay strong (even in our times of weakness and low), and be watchful. For **'The thief does not come except to steal, and to kill and to destroy. I have come that they may have life and that they may have it more abundantly.'** - John 10:10.

Your breakthrough begins now!

This is your time to rise above the heaviness of the past and shine brighter than your history's darkness.

Let's pray.

'Father, in the all-powerful name of Jesus, I tell all fear, all anger, unforgiveness, hurt, shame, guilt, embarrassment, all painful

PART 1: DADLESS...

memories to go and never return. I no longer permit any of these things to have a place, influence, or power in or upon my life. I let go of the unforgiveness that I have held onto. I forgive .... for what they did to me and how they treated me. I refuse to hang on to those harmful thoughts and attitudes. I open my heart and life to you, Father, and ask you to take these destructive things from me. To every emotional and psychological wound and every physical scar I bear, Jesus, I ask you now to carry those burdens and heal me from any and every power they have had over me. I ask your Holy Spirit to come now and heal my heart and heal my mind and bring peace and wholeness to my life. Jesus, come now and deliver me from any evil and destructive power at work in or over my life. Father God, give me insight, understanding, and good judgment about what has happened in my life and recognise and identify any future situations that may arise that would try and bring me down again. Help me make wise choices so I can continue to have freedom and power over anything that would try to devour and destroy me. Father, please forgive me for all my wrongs and where I have hurt people. Thank you for loving me and helping me to live for You in the power of Your Spirit and might. Thank you Father, in Jesus' mighty and precious name, Amen.

I want you to now take some time out to rest and relax. When ready, come back to where you left off and continue journeying through this book. Bless you.

CHAPTER 4: A PERSONAL PERSPECTIVE

Perception is everything. **How you see your father is likely how you will see God and how you respond and interact with Him.** So, sometimes we do require a course correction to help us see things more accurately.

We will look at things from a different point of view to help identify and understand how/why we perceive and relate to God the way we do. This may make a world of difference to you and your situation in seeing, speaking and living differently. The previous activity has more to do with your emotional state and how you feel towards/about your dad and Father God, whereas the following lists have more to do with **what you think** about your dad and Father God.

So now I would like to invite you to make a list of thoughts about your dad. Then, make a second list of your thoughts toward God. Cover the first list when you are done, then begin writing your second list. Then compare the two.

   A. What are your thoughts towards/about your dad?
   B. What are your thoughts towards/about Father God?

PART 1: DADLESS...

LIST A   **LIST B**

How did you go? Are there any repeated words with both lists? Our past experiences will to some degree, affect our present disposition and perceptions about God, our dads, and possibly towards others as well. So, it is good to see where we are at with things. We can recognise where to begin and how to work through our issues. Let me give you an example...

Recently my wife and I sold our house and moved interstate. So, from the first day of deciding to make the move and actually arriving at our new destination, and settling into our new home, it took about eight months. For the time we put our house on the market to sell and for the property to settle, that part took two months. In those two months, I struggled with believing that our house would sell quickly; as the market at the time, houses were selling like hotcakes. I would look around and see houses on our street selling in days or weeks at most, but our house took eight weeks. I know this is not a long time overall. However, an underlying issue made those weeks seem like months to me.

What I was struggling with was not the fact that the house took two months to sell; but rather trusting God to provide a buyer. I felt like I was failing on a daily basis to trust God and that He was going to make provisions for our house to sell and settle.

But something was happening in me that I never saw coming. I had no idea why I was frustrated and struggling to believe God would come through in the first place. Especially after both Carmel and I were impressed by the Holy Spirit that God had spoken to us about a house sale that was going to be quick.

It happened one night when I was telling Carmel about where I was at and my daily challenges and struggles with the whole thing; she said: 'You're probably struggling because your dad didn't provide for you.' I was momentarily stunned. That was a sledgehammer moment for me, and things became clear in that instant.

My experience taught me that I had no one to trust and no one to provide for me and that unconsciously transferred over to Father God. I didn't even see it. And not once did it ever occur to me that I had this issue. When I understood what was happening and why I went through what I did, I made peace with God about it, and my attitude and behaviour changed significantly that night. But I, just like you, are still a work in progress.

Just remember: **A work-in-progress is progress at work.**

A quick prayer...

Lord, You are gracious and kind; please forgive me for my negative attitude toward You. I didn't see the issues in me, and now I see that I need You to work in me, so I can learn to trust in You and honour You. Help me to understand what I don't understand, and for You to change me where I can't or won't. Thank You that You are doing good work for me. I am a new man/person because of this. Thank You.

My Will and Emotion

Human beings are very complex and intricately put together. We are so much more than mere flesh and blood, muscle, etc. From one view, we are simply a bundle of developed and evolved cells with a structure that has survived and lasted the test and harshness of time. There is no real purpose other than to survive and do the best we can to ensure the survival of our existence. Allegedly we were not put here, but we just formed and developed over time in just the right sequence of events at just the right conditions at just the right amount of time at just the right temperature at just the right mix of raw materials at just the right everything that is required not just for life but for the processes and continuation of it.

There is no real meaning or purpose to this existence; we are all just animals with the aim to fight and win over all others to survive. With this view, there is no fixed origin, no satisfying explanation, and no point or purpose to being. There is no meaningful future to look forward to since there is no life beyond what you experience now. This view is quite flawed since one would require all knowledge to know that there is nothing else outside this reality. But no person is omniscient.

You and I are simply a bag of meat with evolved instincts that help us survive; that's it! Does this make you feel special? Unique? Purposeful? Loved? That you are part of something greater? Or that someone is thinking about you? Of course not.

OK, let's take another view.

'You made all the delicate inner parts of my body and knit me together in my mother's womb. Thank you for making me so wonderfully complex! Your workmanship is marvelous - how well I know it. You watched me as I was being formed in utter seclusion, as I was woven together in the dark of the womb. You saw me before I was born. Every day of my life was recorded in Your book. Every moment was laid out before a single day had passed. How precious are Your thoughts about me, O God? They cannot be numbered!' - Psalm 139:13-17.

PART 1: DADLESS...

What do you think about these words? How do these words make you feel?

You were made for a purpose, and Father God loves and cares about you. You were put together in a special one-off design. And the great part is that Jesus puts all human beings on the same level. We are all loved the same, and no one is more loved than another. We are all children of God, and like my mum used to say as we three boys were growing up, 'I love you all the same.'

If you have not experienced it already, God so intensely desires to have a personal relationship with you and for you to experience His care, His love, His favour, His healing touch, His good and fulfilling will for you, His presence, power, promises, provision, protection and purposes.

Let me quickly say this before getting to my point of Will and Emotion. If you have never given your life to Jesus as your Lord and Saviour, now is the time. It is simply putting your faith and trust in Him.

Jesus stands at the door of your heart and knocks; you hear the knock but don't know how to respond or what to do. From your heart, in your own words, ask Him to come into your life, forgive you of your sins, ask Him to make you a new person and for His daily presence, help and healing.

I know when I decided to invite Jesus to be Lord in my life, it went something like this:

Jesus, forgive me of my sins; I need you in my life; help me to live for you. Show me Your purpose for me. Amen. Since then,

God has revealed Himself to me and shown Himself in different ways, ever faithfully. I want to share more about this in the next part of this book.

You know, when you make Jesus 'Lord' of your life, what you're doing is surrendering to Him, yielding to His call on your life and saying, 'I have lived life my way, and it hasn't turned out good at all and I am sorry for this. I need You to come into my life and situation and turn things around. You have an excellent plan for my life, and I want to know this, live for you with trust and faith. I don't understand everything but help me to live with your wisdom and strength. Give me peace where I have had turmoil and healing where I have had wounds. Give me wholeness where I have only known helplessness and brokenness. Give me love and comfort where I only know abuse, hate and loneliness. Please give me a future and hope where I only have despair and discouragement. Turn my life around only as You can and transform me into the person You always intended me to be. Father God, please take over and change my life in every way.

There are other things as well. Things like: When Jesus comes into your life, your eternal destiny is changed, and your life here and now takes on a whole new direction and meaning.

He is now the Lord of your life, which means He is responsible for you. He will look after you, provide for you, counsel you by His Holy Spirit, and help you see the world differently, think differently and live differently. He wants to show you how much He loves and cares about you. You are special to Him, and He, God, '**...saved you by His grace when you believed.**' - Ephesians 2:8.

The truth is that in life, people will hurt you, offend you, and bring negative things your way. But take heart; you are no longer alone or powerless to handle and overcome (not just survive) whatever comes your way. We must begin to thank God through all situations, not for bad situations, but to know that He is with us through everything that will come our way.

And believe me when I say, **'We know that God causes everything to work together for the good of those who love God and are called according to His purpose for them.'** - Romans 8:28.

Father God sees what you don't see and cannot see. He knows what is coming up; He knows all things, and nothing surprises Him. He knows your needs even before you need those things. He makes a way where there seems to be no way. He opens doors that cannot be shut and shuts doors that cannot be opened. Whether these things are events, opportunities or past occurrences. We must seek Him every day and wait for Him to speak with us, and He wants us to enjoy His presence. Jesus came to give you a fulfilling, healthy, blessed, purposeful, significant, meaningful, abundant and joyful life.

A Small Sidestep

A story I want to tell you is one of God, one day, standing outside a building with a rather large umbrella. It is pouring rain outside, but He is dry as a bone. All the people not under His umbrella are getting drenched from all the heavy rain. They seem to be running somewhere but not really going anywhere in particular. They are all running in random patterns, seemingly in a panic, thinking they are getting closer to undercover from the rain. The rain is so heavy that it is difficult to see where they are going, and it is also tough to hear anything else because of the noise the rain is making as it hits the street and other buildings and vehicles.

Then, God calls out to those running aimlessly, and it seems they either ignore Him or seem to believe that they know where they are going. But as time goes on, it is clear that these people are getting nowhere but only more saturated in the rain. But finally, someone looks up and sees God standing under His large umbrella, all dry and calm, gesturing to him to come under His umbrella to escape the rain. The man refuses and thinks he can find a closer and better place of refuge. He keeps on searching. God calls out to another man and sees Him, but he keeps looking and scampering around for cover. Time and time again, God calls out to the people running and scrambling for protection from the storm. But no one comes. But God is not deterred; he persists in calling out and making Himself available to everyone willing to come under His umbrella.

Finally, after calling out to many people, God gets a response. The young man quickly but cautiously runs over but still stands out in the rain. He hastily questions God, 'Why are you standing out in the rain, under Your large umbrella, and what's the catch?' But just as God was about to reply, the man hurriedly ran off and continued looking for shelter. Undeterred, God remains outside, holding up His umbrella, waiting for someone to accept His offer of cover and protection.

At last, an older gentleman shuffles over to meet with God and asks Him if it would be ok to stand under His umbrella, God welcomes the man in, and the older man stands close to God under His umbrella, out of the rain. A person standing on the other side of the street notices this and quickly runs over and does the same. And so, another, then another. Before long, many people were standing under God's umbrella, but God's umbrella was so big that there was room for all, but not everyone took up His offer.

When there is a need in your life, God is present to aid you. He knew of your need before you did and offered you and me a way out and exactly what we required at the right time. When we come in under God's covering, we have the blessings of everything He wants to give. When we step out from His coverage, we fall into trouble and potentially on a path that is not good for us in this life and possibly for eternity. Here is a truth about salvation: When a human being has not yet received Jesus into their life, there is a legal issue of ownership. We do not yet belong to God until we step in under His lordship and ownership. His grace saves us through faith in His Son. This means that the real enemy of people, Satan and his cronies, has legal access and rights to you and me. They may not possess us, but we can be influenced by spirits when we are not in the perfect will of God. We are not under His protection or legally His. It is just like a court of law. We are guilty before God because of sin. Christ, our advocate, is defending us and making a case for our acquittal. The Devil is our adversary and accuser, trying to make a case (and lies) against you and me to see us condemned with the worst form of punishment — darkness, pain and separation from God.

But, our advocate, our mediator, the Lord Jesus, has taken the fall for us — Himself. He offered up His own life as a man so He could die and defeat the Devil at His own game, rise from the dead, and have total victory and authority over death and sin and its consequences. As human beings, we are now in a unique position that even the angels are not entitled to – salvation! Then, when you ask Jesus to come into your life and to change you and renew you through Jesus' blood, you are forgiven of all sin as Christ has taken them away and we are as righteous as Christ through faith and repentance in Him. As you take these steps, you now have the Spirit of Christ living in you, and the Holy Spirit is in your spirit and is now part of your life. This is what it means to be born again. And this must take place in you, so you can legally enter God's great domain, His kingdom. His presence.

God the Father understands that with our human imperfections, we do stuff up on our journey of His ongoing work within us. This is not a permission, loophole or license to go and do the former things you may have gotten into. He wants us to live the kind of life Christ exemplified. But God, in His love and grace, faithfulness, and goodness, knows our daily struggles. He gave us His Holy Spirit to help us, to guide and counsel us, to convict us of sin, to enable and empower us, to strengthen us, to transform us, to refine us, to encourage us, build us and to appoint us to fulfill His mission, plans and purposes – His good, pleasing and perfect will.

If you are not under The Lord's umbrella, go there. If you are under the Lord's umbrella, stay there; if you feel that you may have stepped out from under His umbrella, then it is time to get right with Him and get back to that place of a close relationship. Don't be bought out by the lure or illusion of missing out or that better things are out there.

'He (the Devil) was a murderer from the beginning. He has always hated the truth because there is no truth in him. When

PART 1: DADLESS...

he lies, it is consistent with his character; for he is a liar and the father of lies.' - John 8:44.

Returning to the main focus of MY WILL AND EMOTIONS, The Holy Spirit is constantly at work within you. Here is a remarkable promise: **'And I am certain that God, who began the good work within you, will continue His work until it is finally finished on the day when Christ Jesus returns.'** - Philippians 1:6.

My Commitment

A PROMPT TO PERSIST

A few years ago, when I met with my half-sister, we sat around a table at a cafe and talked about all kinds of things which was meaningful. And though I don't remember everything we talked about, there is one thing I will never forget from that day: the picture she showed me on her phone. It was a picture of my dad with his other son (my half-brother) and his (my brothers') good friend. The shot was taken of them in a boat, holding a huge barramundi fish, showing off their 'trophy' catch. It looked like a happy and prize-winning moment. When I saw my brothers' friend standing in the boat holding up the prized catch with jubilation, I said, 'That should have been me standing there, not some family friend.' This was my thought.

After seeing that picture, I was pretty let down and resentful for quite some time. It really got to me because deep down, I was still craving that kind of relationship and sharing those types of experiences with my dad, and not some stranger getting it all. Seeing that picture accentuated what was already resident within me. It brought to the surface and magnified what I was then dealing with. It wasn't a setback but a setup (though I didn't see this at the time) to cause me to see that there was still much hurt, disappointment, resentment, anger and craving from which God wanted to free me from.

I had to refocus on the giver, not the taker of my joy.

It is very easy to go day to daily with no real effort on our part, to dwell on the hurtful, harmful and negative events and emotions of the past; it can be somewhat of an automatic experience. But I do realise it is sometimes just too painful and emotional to confront and deal with, so we choose avoidance instead. With this course of action, though, I have never seen anyone truly or significantly recover or break free from hurt, loss, grief or another debilitating personal life anchor.

Let me say one thing here: don't go it alone! Many times throughout my life, I have looked back and remembered all the good people God put in my life at just the right time to help me out of a situation or guide me through a situation. Your first and foremost guidance will come from God's Holy Spirit, His Word and through His people. I have asked Father God to show me many times depending on where I am at in life and what is happening at the time; 'Show me in Your word where I can get some help, some guidance, some confirmation, some understanding, some relatability, some answers, some comfort, some truth, some connection, some clarity, some encouragement, some strengthening, some reinforcement, some healing, some joy.' In short, here are some answers!

God will send help your way. God hears and answers prayer. The Old Testament account where King Hezekiah reached out to the Lord was real to him then and is true for us now. He

PART 1: DADLESS...

replied: **'I have heard your prayer and seen your tears; I will heal you.'** - 2 Kings 20:5.

If it is not God's desire to heal you, why would He send His own Son to a meager life, an atrocious punishment, and then meet a gruesome death? **'But He was pierced for our rebellion, crushed for our sins. He was beaten so we could be whole. He was whipped so we could be healed.'** - Isaiah 53:5.

Let me encourage you with this simple but powerful analogy...

I wanted to plant some vegetables in my backyard at home. So, I pulled together several large containers, pots and tubs for the garden beds. I bought all the packets of seeds that I needed and selected ten different vegetables. I wanted to start from scratch and get the best out of what I planted. It was far easier to plant from seedlings, but I wanted to challenge myself and do it all from scratch, the very basics.

I prepared the soil, planted the seeds according to the recommendations, and watered and put on 'plant food' to help the seeds sprout, grow, and flourish. To ultimately produce a much-anticipated harvest. Weeks and months went by with no fruit, and even though there was plenty of growth and development, the fruit was lacking. I wasn't going to be deterred about this, so I persisted with watering and maintaining the vegetable garden. After many weeks, I started to ask, 'where is the fruit I am supposed to get?' I give water, net protection from the birds, and plant food for growth and development, but where is the harvest of fruit I was expecting? All I see are growing green plants without fruit. But, finally, after months of care, determination and persistence, I began to see some tomatoes, baby beets, carrots, onions, a cucumber and also other vegetables. It took so long,

83

and the crops were slowly becoming fruitful. A couple of times a week, I picked various vegetables and enjoyed the fruit of my labour; natural, healthy and beneficial for my body.

We must put our hand on the plow and not look back. **Yield to be Healed.** Continue to move forward with the end in mind. When you look at the Cross of Christ, you could look at it with the perspective of violence, brutality, gruesome, and ultimately, death. And this is an accurate viewpoint. However, another view is conversely true; the full picture of the Cross (as mentioned previously) has a twofold nature. It is a tool for torture and death, yet it symbolises life and freedom. Christ had to die to give/provide life for others, the whole world. Just as a seed must first die, it then has the capacity for life and fruitfulness.

When you went through your times of harshness, harm, loss, abuse, loneliness, isolation, grief and other terrible things, your life was being plowed, and there was a breaking of the ground, of your heart and soul. These, too, have a two-fold nature. Your experiences as your body and soul were being plowed open from adverse events and words allowed Father God to plant seeds of hope, life, truth, restoration, healing, blessing and other good things; to be planted within you.

A seemingly negative and broken picture now has the perfect setting for our heavenly Father to plant, cover, water, nourish and care for our whole life, wellbeing, and future because God wants to have a very fruitful and whole person that is specially selected and picked for healing and for His purposes.

But God demonstrates His own love for us in this: While we were still sinners, Christ died for us.' - Romans 5:8.

Transition Can Be Tough

People prefer the outcome of change (good/positive change) but not necessarily the process of change. Change can be hard, not easily adaptable and often difficult. It upheaves your life and frequently demands uncomfortableness and differences not necessarily wanted or anticipated. From now on, life will be different, no longer the same.

It is too easy and tempting sometimes to want to stay in the past, keep things as they were, and not be open to embracing new things. However, all this sounds somewhat negative. But life is full of change, not all bad or negative. See the change in your life as new healing, new direction, new opportunities, new life appointments, new friendships, new attitudes, new wholeness, new skills, new knowledge, new abilities, new income, new environment, new blessings, new solutions, new living arrangements, new development, new business, new health, new influence, new interests, new conversations, new life.

It still holds; if you want pure metal, you must first refine it. The refining fires are hot, and the refining methods and processes are long, carefully and strategically done. Sometimes you start your day and seem to be in an 'off-centre' kind of place, and every person around you is stupid today. They do things to fire you up, annoy and agitate you. And you think to yourself, 'What's wrong with these people today?' Is it them, or is it just me? Sometimes it's both. LOL! My point is that there may be something underlying that may be at play.

At times it can feel like you are being dragged over the hot coals, and things seem like a breeze on other days. There will be times when your hurts and grief from the past are in your life; you know they are there, but you do your best to avoid or deny them any chance of getting in your face. The very thought of dealing with your emotional past is not what you want to confront and be intentional in dealing with because the pain you squash down or put to the side of your life is just too painful. The truth is that wherever you go, you cannot escape yourself.

God's Holy Spirit can do more in a single moment for you than in a lifetime of doing things in your own strength and abilities that you could ever do. Do you trust Father God to love you unconditionally and do personal and powerful work in you (even though other people who you may or may not know) to at least establish and even help take you through your refining fires? The three young men in the fiery furnace described in the book of Daniel were seen walking around in the fire unharmed and with a fourth person, taking them through and protecting them through the potential life-taking event. God is with you through the fires and refining of your life. It can be fearful or frustrating, but you will be a transformed whole person at the end of such things.

God intends to meet with your permission to show you He can be trusted. The Holy Spirit has everything you need to help you become a brand-new person that no longer has to suffer, no longer has to have a sense of hopelessness or despair, or feels imprisoned with fear, hurt, anger, unforgiveness, mistrust, anxiety, abuse or betrayal.

Father God wants to take out the sting from your past and put in His peace for your present and future. He can do this for you now. James 4:8 says: **'Draw near to God, and He will draw near to you.'**

Expect a Fight

If you hadn't noticed, there are two beings out to get you. One is Father God; the other is Satan, the father of lies. The first is about giving you freedom and abundant life. The second is about taking from you all he can and making your life as broken and miserable as possible. God comes to give life; Satan comes to take life. John 10:10 says, **'The thief's purpose is to steal and kill and destroy.'** Is it any wonder when you start to get things going well in your life, your walk with the Lord is getting closer, or perhaps you have been given new responsibilities in your church or mission field/calling; something 'crops up,' totally left field?

It could be sickness all of a sudden running rampant in your family. There are new difficulties or challenges or even old or new temptations in your life. Someone wrongs you or legally brings a suit against you. Maybe your reputation or name is being tarnished. Someone may be trying to fabricate some allegation against you. Close relationships are a bit rocky now, or out of the blue situations/circumstances are now plaguing you. Take heart!

Big wins come from big challenges.

'Because the Spirit who lives in you is greater than the spirit who lives in the world.' - 1 John 4:4.

Keep in mind that God's word says we are to **'Stay alert! Watch out for your great enemy, the Devil. He prowls around like a roaring lion, looking for someone to devour.'** He is bent on taking you down. If you are a believer and follower of Jesus Christ, you are his target. Satan and his cronies will aim to bring confusion, delay and issue your way to put you off your game, distract you, and plant doubt and fear in your thoughts and heart. This is why it is so important to discern, perceive, identify or recognise what is happening around you or even to you. Situational awareness is important to know what is occurring and understand it.

Our enemy is spiritual and knowing his tactics is vital in having a defense and victory over him. **'But thank God! He gives us victory over sin and death through our Lord Jesus Christ.'** - 1 Corinthians 15:57.

A side prayer...

Father God, help me to see and recognise Your plans and purposes for my life and to recognise and discern the schemes and strategies of the enemy. Help me to trust in You and Your word whenever these things arise so I can live in victory in every situation. In Jesus' mighty name.

A word of intent...

BEGIN YOUR JOURNEY!

STAY THE COURSE!

SEE IT THROUGH!

BE ENCOURAGED, GOD IS WITH YOU, AND HE WILL SEE IT THROUGH TO THE END!

'The end of a thing is better than its beginning.' - Ecclesiastes 7:8.

My Thoughts and Words

Amongst the many important things, our thoughts and words are high on the list for keeping an eye on and for transformation. A change of mind can happen instantly; more often than not, we can say things that are complete opposites in the same breath. Part of God's restoration work in us is being transformed not only with our words but by our thinking as well, and this is where the Devil, or Devils, are attacking us the most. This transformation is a two-way effort.

In order for change to take place, we must **'...let God transform (us) you into a new person by changing the way you (we) think.' - Romans 12:2. A change of thought is a change of perspective and a change of view is a change of attitude. A shift in mindset is a change of behaviour, and a change of behaviour is a change of life.**

Now let's make this relevant for you. Making your bed every morning. How do you go with this? Do you look at this as a menial, boring or superficial task? Or do you look at this as an act of self-discipline, creating structure and routine in your day and life?

Making your bed is a means to a purpose. But as we look differently at things, we see more at work. Establishing effective practices in your life brings short-term and long-term benefits. I am saying that when we are in the process of change, it is very easy to allow the wheels to fall off and simply quit. Sometimes you will feel that things are hard, and at times they will be. Sometimes you will think that there is no fruit or accomplishment with your actions. Sometimes you will think that all of what you are doing is fruitless, pointless, meaningless, and outright just a waste of your time and effort. But hang on.

Think first before you act!

It is simpler, easier and quicker to quit, but at what cost? What is on the line in your life if you were to stop now? What would your life look like next month or next year if you continued your transformation journey? That said, it is equally important to not only keep tabs on your daily choices but also watch the daily content of your thoughts. One thing I learnt while working in the High-Risk Work and Work Health and Safety industry is the implementation, monitoring, and reviewing of protection and prevention measures to help mitigate the dangers and risks to help protect your and others' time while on the work site. Injury prevention is key to a safe and healthy work life.

So, for example, three elements can cause short-term or possibly permanent injury while performing a task.

They are:

1. **Frequency** - How often?
2. **Repetition** - How many times?
3. **Duration** - How long?

I want you to apply these questions to yourself in your day. Particularly if you have doubt when tempted, have harmful thoughts, or other thoughts that may hinder or block the progress of your journey. Be aware of your thoughts and the content of them. Are you receiving any thoughts against or contrary to what the Bible says? Or to any words you may have received from reading the word of God or by others praying for you and what they have said. Our thoughts can sometimes put us off track or keep us off track if we allow certain thoughts or distortions of the truth, which can become 'truth.'

- How often do I have these specific thoughts?
- How many times would you go over these particular thoughts?
- How long would you think about these things?

Our past or present experiences can either enslave us or free us. In the movie 'The Hurricane,' Denzel Washington plays the part of Rubin 'Hurricane' Carter, and he says:

'Hate put me in prison; love's gonna bust me out.' Your enemy, our enemy (which will be unique/common to each of us), wants us to be prison bound, but Father God sent Jesus, his only son, to free us and redeem us from the power and influence of those enemies. If you believe you are trapped and there is no way out of your situation, and there seems to be no way out (in your current belief) or fear is keeping you bound, then know that God came to rescue you, liberate you and heal you of your current situation. **'And they have defeated him by the blood of the lamb and by their testimony.'** - Revelation 13:11.

Just remember, Satan twists and contorts the truth with a lie or partial truths. He won't influence or manipulate you with an outright lie; he will slowly and cunningly, over time, enmesh his lies and deceptions with your thoughts. So over time, truths are replaced with outright lies. And with these strategies and weapons of his, beliefs and perspectives are entrenched into our very consciousness. We then live out of these beliefs, which negatively impact our lives and how we live with others. They can also cause us to believe that we are beyond help or that God cannot help or heal us.

The only way we can know for sure what is going on and to what extent the damage there is, is with the intervention and help of the Holy Spirit (for He is the Spirit of Truth. So, whatever He says is truth) and, of course, the word of God.

CHAPTER 5: BE WATCHFUL

I want to say something which I trust is encouraging for you, and it is hoped that what you are about to read will strengthen and motivate you to take positive and intentional action. I have every reason these words will.

'So Christ has truly set us free. Now make sure that you stay free, and don't get tied up again in slavery to the law.' - Galatians 5:1.

I am saying that when the Lord is doing or has done a work in your life, avoid slipping into a rut or going backward in your freedom. Let me give you a scriptural account, and I'll make it relevant to you. But first…

'Let us strip off every weight that slows us down, especially the sin that so easily trips us up. And let us run with endurance the race God has set before us.' - Hebrews 12:1.

Do you remember the story in Matthew 12:43-45 where a man went through a 'spiritual clean-out'? Jesus was referring to the attitude of the nation of Israel, which is true for us in our daily relationship with the Lord. He was liberated from his demonic captor, but what happened then was the worst thing for that man. Sometime after his release, he was again besieged by that same demon and seven others! He was far worse off now than at the beginning of his ordeal.

There are a few things to consider here.

1. Only the Spirit of God can do certain things that you cannot do in your own strength and ability.
2. When you have a 'spiritual clean-out,' you may be freed but you must be filled with His word and Holy Spirit.
3. Reorient yourself to following God, as a non-moving and 'cleaned out' person is now a target for Satan/his entourage.

CHAPTER 6: GOING FORWARD

When Peter was in prison (Acts 12:6-10), **'...suddenly there was a bright light in the cell, and an angel of the Lord stood before Peter. The angel struck him on the side to awaken him and said, 'Quick! Get up!' And the chains fell off his wrists.'**

There will, of course, be times in our life when we will experience different seasons; remember, they are seasons and not permanents. God can and does beautiful things in and through us and even when we are doing the right things, we can sometimes feel alone, isolated, bound, or even stuck or discouraged about what is happening or what may not be happening.

I believe God wants to say to you now that if you are feeling any of the above emotions or having thoughts that are not in line with His word, like; 'you can do all things through Christ who gives you strength, or 'you have authority over the enemy, 'God will fight for you, 'the fight is the Lords', The Holy Spirit is the counselor and He will speak to you and guide you into all truth. His Holy Spirit wants to get before you, shine His light on you and get your attention. He wants to move on you, and He will show you the way out of that dark dungeon and tunnel.

It is time for you to rise up in His enabling power and finally and forever walk in victory, favour and freedom with purpose! Those chains are broken off your life now in Jesus' name and they no longer have any power over you!

Chains of depression to fall to the ground!

Chains of feeling like a failure to fall to the ground!

Chains of fear fall to the ground!

Chains of the hardness of heart to fall to the ground!

Chains of unforgiveness fall to the ground!

Chains of wrong and faulty thinking fall to the ground!

Chains of sinful behaviour to fall to the ground!

Chains of harsh and hurtful words fall to the ground!

Chains of the power of others' words to fall to the ground!

Chains of demonic power fall to the ground!

Chains of unhealthy and toxic relationships to end and fall to the ground!

Chains of ungodly spiritual, emotional, and soul ties fall to the ground!

Chains of procrastination fall to the ground!

Chains of indifference and apathy fall to the ground!

Chains of adultery to fall to the ground!

Chains of anything that I put before God to fall to the ground!

Chains of pride and ego fall to the ground!

Chains of unhealthy grief to fall to the ground!

IN JESUS NAME!!

Take heart, God is on your side, and His will for you is good. He is faithful. Every step you take with Him is moving you forward into His plans and purposes, especially for you. **'The Lord says, 'I will guide you along the best pathway for your life. I will advise you and watch over you.'** - Psalm 32:8.

CHAPTER 7: LEARNING FROM GOD IN DIFFICULT TIMES

One thing's for sure is when you start your journey and allow God to work in your soul/mind, body and spirit and situations, you will begin to recognise what God does for us, and He shows us what He is really like. You will start to see Him for who He is and begin to see what you really are. When you put a tea bag into boiling water, the water draws out what is inside the leaves. It's similar to noting that when the Lord starts to do a work in you, you begin to see what is in you.

Be encouraged; what you see today is not the finished product. No building site looks great at any time when construction is in progress, or a renovation, for that matter. **When God does a work in a person, He doesn't leave them a hole; He leaves them whole.** You may not like what you see in yourself at certain times of your journey, but God loves you anyhow, and He sees Jesus in you and the finished work.

Whatever seems to feel or look unpleasant or bad, Father God is about transformation, not deformation. Take, for example, the potter's wheel in Jeremiah 18. We are in the Lord's hands, and He has a plan to shape and form us into His wonderful image for a specific purpose. We cannot form ourselves. We cannot do the work only the Lord Himself can do.

PART 1: DADLESS...

Let me give some examples of men who we would assume to 'have it all together' but started off on somewhat shaky ground and fell short of perfection. But ultimately, they did what God had appointed for them. Maybe you can identify or relate with one or more of these men of faith, just as I do.

By the way, failing or even running from God doesn't make you an evil or terrible person; it might mean that you're in the process of getting to that place where you're ready to deal with and agree with God and His plans and redemption for your life. Remember, Father God loves and cares about you and wants the very best for you as only He can give. He wants you to achieve great things.

1. **Moses**: Even though He ran from his first home in fear of being caught for murdering a slave taskmaster, he ran off into the desert for forty years before he responded to the Lord and was ready for the next chapter of his life. He led millions of people in a nation to freedom, but not without his flaws and failings. He disobeyed God; he had a speech impediment, fear, and reservations about what God was calling him to do. He was intimidated by the immensity of the task set before him. **The size of the task before you is not as great as the size of the God within you**. Even though Moses had fears, failings, frailties and flaws, he also had faith and faithfulness to see through God's appointment for him to the end.

2. **Gideon**: The Lord sought this guy out. If God wants you, His plans will stand, and He will have the last say. In his mind and by his tongue, Gideon believed and stated that he had loads of fear, was in hiding, and was the weakest of his tribe and of his family. The angel of the Lord simply

said to Gideon, **'Mighty hero, the Lord is with you.'** The Lord also said to him, **'Go with the strength you have...I am sending you!'** The angel of the Lord then did a miracle in front of Gideon, and still, after this, Gideon asked for two other signs to confirm if God was truly going to use him for this particular mission. In our imperfect and incomplete perspective, it is impossible to understand who we are and what we could become accurately.

3. **Jonah:** God had appointed this man to tell the people of Nineveh to repent, get right with God, and do away with all their sinful and godless practices and lifestyles. But Jonah got angry because he knew that even with all these peoples' problems and rebellion towards God, God would forgive them and restore them unto Himself. So, Jonah went in the opposite direction, and he ran away from the voice and vocation of the Lord. God would have His will done, and no man or system can stop that. Jonah eventually found himself in a whale and vomited up on shore three days later. He finally turned towards the Lord and went about His business. We sometimes get in the way of our destiny. But God has a way of getting our attention and getting us back on board for His perfect purpose. You must also remember; God is gracious to us even when He is not obligated to be.

4. **David:** This man had a rap sheet probably longer than most. David stuffed up and sinned so much that God's love for him still didn't change. Conspiring to murder, adultery, for example. But, **The love of God is greater than the sin of man**. God is justified in dealing with all of us swiftly, but when you get to know Him more personally and profoundly, you soon realise that He is more than a Spirit 'up there somewhere.'

The blame game began when things started with Adam and Eve. Blame shifting and finger-pointing were going on everywhere. Someone else was deemed guilty, so they could feel better about themselves and feel justified about their disobedient actions. Eve said, 'The serpent deceived me....' Adam said to the Lord, 'The woman You gave me....' No one wanted to be held accountable. For human beings, this was the first instance where fear and trembling were experienced. As well as guilt and shame. But God is the same yesterday, today and forever. He is faithful, fair, righteous, wise, good, loving, powerful, gracious, merciful, holy and so much more.

So, David had his share of wrongdoing, but he also had a heart and desire after God. He did great things for the Lord.

5. **Levi (Matthew):** The worst occupation of the time. No one liked these people because they were corrupt and scammed people with their hard-earned money. Tax collectors were intensely despised. But this is one of the men whom Jesus wanted on His team. **Father God doesn't choose us based on how good we are but on how good He is**. Matthew ended up writing the gospel of Matthew. Even though this man was called, he had to choose to follow and become a disciple of Jesus. He took up an offer he could not refuse. This is necessary to the idea that **'partnership'** is crucial for a new life in Christ.

Whatever your background, we all need to be saved from ourselves and an eternity that is separate from God. When you heed the call and respond to Jesus, life is for the taking, and He has promised to be with you every step of the way.

So, how do you see yourself? Do you see yourself as weak, fearful, with no back or steel, or feeling/believing like you're the least? It's easy and natural to look and see ourselves through our own eyes, but we must transition to seeing ourselves through Father's eyes. The question is, how do we begin to see ourselves through God's eyes?

One key to this answer is **PARTNERSHIP**. God came down to earth, so we must reach up to heaven. Following are some elements I believe are critical in helping us see ourselves as He sees us. There will, of course, be other factors.

1. **Love of God:** Nothing can separate us from the love of God. No person, sin, shame, guilt, power, distance or situation can keep you and me apart from the immense and unconditional love of the Father. Sometimes I wonder if all the adverse circumstances in this life are there to show humanity how good and great God truly is. **God does not love us for our sins; He loves us despite our sins.**

    He first loved us while we were still sinners. The very fact that we are aware of our flaws, weaknesses and godless propensities; shows us beyond any doubt that even though God very well knows who we are and why we do the things we do, God still loves us anyhow. **There is nothing you can do to make God love you more.**

    There is also nothing more Jesus could do to make you right with Him.

    We are in a hopeless situation without Him. But Jesus did what we could not do. And it is by this act of love that God the Father did the complete opposite of what mere humans would do.

I'll explain.

God made man/woman; they willingly did the wrong thing by God. The reasonable and justifiable response to this act was death and separation from God. But God was gracious and merciful. Man sinned, and God was merciful. God gave hope to humanity and still does through His Son. We are saved by grace through faith. His blood redeems us. God forgave when He didn't have to. We blame God or get angry at Him for many things, yet God chose to love sinners and offer them a way out of their sins, His Son.

We get angry at God for Him allowing certain things to happen. But also let us have free will, and there are consequences for free will choices. Death, disease, corruption, broken relationships and so on. How can we blame God, who didn't make the choices we blame Him for in the first place? Humanity makes decisions every day that impacts our future positively or negatively. Either way, **we harvest what we plant**.

God made a way out of our mess. Our mess! We must realise that God is at our side whenever we invite Him to be involved. This is one of His promises. Jesus stands at the door of your heart, knocking to get your attention. Will you let Him in? He's waiting for you to answer.

2. **Spirit of God**: Unless we have the Spirit of Christ, we are not God's children; we do not belong to Him. If we do not belong to Him, we are not His property. He is not our king. We are then an open game for the Devil and his cronies for the taking. There is neither no protection nor covering. Because we are mere humans, mere mortals, it is impossible to accomplish the works and deeds of

the spirit if we do not have His Spirit within us. There is a chasm between Him and us that only Christ can bridge. God's Spirit must be living inside us, connected with our spirit to receive His restoration, blessing, favour, healing and relationship.

3. **Word of God**: The word of God is more than just words on paper or a screen. **'In the beginning, the Word already existed. The Word was with God, and the Word was God. He existed in the beginning with God. God created everything through Him, and nothing was created except through Him. The Word gave life to everything that was created, and His life brought light to everyone.'** - John 1:1-4.

'So the Word became human and made His home among us. He was full of unfailing love and faithfulness. And we have seen His glory, the glory of the Father's one and only Son.' - John 1:14.

Jesus is the Son of God, and He is the Word of God.

'For the Word of God is alive and powerful. It is sharper than the sharpest two-edged sword, cutting between soul and spirit, between joint and marrow. It exposes our innermost thoughts and desires. Nothing in creation is hidden from God. Everything is naked and exposed before His eyes, and He is the one to whom we are accountable.' - Hebrews 4:12-13.

We need the Word of God present in us for true life and holiness. We must have physical food, spirit and soul food to live and grow, know God, and know what is required of us.

Without the Word of God, we are lifeless. The Word of God is what helps us to do life better. The Word of God teaches us life lessons; it gives us knowledge, wisdom, insight, understanding, and enhancement. The Spirit and Word of God must be present for us to succeed and be freed.

Every person alive has the same amount of time every day, week, month and year. You have 168 hours per week, so how will you spend your time? **Reading and learning/understanding the word of God can be either a religious act or a spiritual experience**. Going through the motions is as lifeless as you could make it. However, letting the Word of God transform you is a different matter.

Here is my usual custom:

- I get on my own
- I pray that every other voice or distraction will cease and go (In Jesus' name)
- I start to thank the Lord/show gratitude
- I ask for deep understanding and insight as I read the Word
- I ask the Lord to speak to me and show me new things and how it is relevant
- I write down/date what I sense God is saying to me
- I thank Him and wait for a while to see what else He wants to say.

This is the general way I come to God and get into His Word. Though, it varies on occasion. I constantly endeavour not to get religious about reading or spending time with Father God. In other words, go into that time with faith, expecting God to speak to you. Do read his word, ask Him to guide you where to read next, and have the plan to go through, or you may find that you will miss a day, then a week, then several weeks have slipped by without you even picking up the Bible. Also, focus on getting to know Him, getting closer to Him, and having a more profound and personal face-to-face experience with Him.

You may already have your own way of doing things, and this is good, keep it personal and unique. I also try to have some morning time and evening time on a daily basis. God knows your situation, so be as regular as possible, even for a short time when / where you can. Believe Father for that to change and that your current circumstance will allow you to engage in more continuous and significant times with Him.

I have found that shifting your focus on Him rather than what you want from Him is healthier for you, and you can avoid disappointment. God wants to answer your prayers, but His timeline and how He answers your prayers is somewhat different from our timeline and what those answered prayers will look like. Understand that He does know more and sees further than we ever could. We must trust in His infinite wisdom and knowledge about us and the very things we are praying and believing for.

I have also discovered that I must be persistent in my faith and patience. Being persistent in having faith in Him and following His guidance and instruction in His word will help me stay on track with trusting Him with my desires and dreams so that He can bring them to pass and get clarity and confirmation along the way.

Here is something else that has helped me immensely; Be persistent with your patience. It is important to believe and trust in God and to persist in staying the course and persevering with your patience in the waiting. **Waiting is an act of faith**. Grow while you wait.

'Be still, and know that I am God!' - Psalms 46:10.

The more you position yourself to know God personally (and not just about Him) your journey will be one of less striving, impatience, stress, worry, or any other faithless or negative experience you may go through. The more time you spend with someone, the better you get to know them, and the closer you will be. This is true of your relationship with the Father as well.

If you struggle with waiting, reading the word, or hearing from Him, ask someone you know who can pray with you, get around people who rub shoulders with Him often and be around faith-filled people and those who encourage you and help you on your journey. I believe that you will get the breakthrough you are seeking. He wants to connect with you on a more personal and profound level.

Ask, seek, knock and repeat the process. There's something else: Be confident with God's peace in your heart, that settledness, that inner and deep knowing. That intrinsic/inherent Holy Spirit witnesses restfulness, calmness, peacefulness, quiet, and hush. Your conscience is at ease. There is a resonance between your spirit/soul and the Holy Spirit.

When you hear from God's word and the personal utterance and revelation of the Holy Spirit, you understand that the Spirit of Truth is in your being, and His voice and knowledge is giving you peace that didn't come from your situation or others or yourself. When you get this, you can move forward in the things before you to do with His backing, blessing and boldness.

This wonders for your faith, for faith comes from hearing God's word. We can hear audibly, by our spirit, by the Holy Spirit, by the spoken word of others, by a confirming sign, by circumstances, by miracles, by healing, by blessing, and by testimony, to name some.

There is one saying that I don't hold to, and it is: Trust your heart; what is your heart saying, go with your heart. If people mean the Bible, the Holy Spirit, and the audible voice of God, then sure. But keep this truth in mind: **'The heart is deceitful above all things, and desperately wicked (or incurably sick).'** - Jeremiah 17:9.

Can or should we then trust our hearts? Apparently not. How can we trust what is inherently broken and corrupt? What does God's word say about God's word and trusting in that? **'Your word is a lamp to guide my feet and a light for my path.'** - Psalm 119:105.

And what about the Holy Spirit?

'When He, the Spirit of truth (the Holy Spirit) has come, He will guide you into all truth; for He will not speak on His own authority, but whatever He hears He will speak; and He will tell you things to come.' - John 16:13.

Let me tell you some other important things about the Word of God.

As we have it today, all 66 books, the Bible **is God's word**! Lock, stock and barrel! **'All Scripture is inspired by God and is useful to teach us what is true and to make us realise what is wrong in our lives. It corrects us when we are wrong and teaches us to do what is right. God uses it to prepare and equip His people to do every good work.'** - 2 Timothy 3:16-17.

Never under-read, undervalue or underestimate the holy, living and powerful word of God. **Apply the word to yourself and yourself to the word.**

> A. **Power / Anointing of God:** Protect God's anointing over your life. Guard it. Foster it. What do I mean? When God calls you, He sets you apart; He has gifts and plans for you. When you are doing the supernatural work of God, when He enables you to carry out 'spiritual works,' you are fulfilling the Father's good and perfect will.
>
> When Jesus went about doing the will of the Father, He operated in the power and authority of the Holy Spirit. **'God anointed (by way of contact) Jesus of Nazareth with the Holy Spirit and with power, who went about doing good and healing all who were oppressed by the Devil, for God was with Him.'** - Acts 10:38.
>
> In the same way, you and I, when we receive by faith, **'you will receive power when the Holy Spirit comes upon you.'** - Acts 1:8.
>
> B. **Blood of Jesus:** All humanity is lost without the blood of Jesus. There is no forgiveness of sin and hell; separation is our eternal lot. And God is justified, righteous and fair with this reality. For the wages of sin is death. God

is holy and perfect; in Him, there is no darkness. To be recipients of God's undeserved favour and love, grace and mercy, we must change our hearts and minds and turn our lives towards Him (by repenting (and turning towards Him) with faith) and make Him the first place in our life. God the Father, Jesus the Son and the Holy Spirit have already done their part; it is now up to us to do our part for connection and redemption.

So, what does the blood of Jesus do for us?

1. **Redeems us**: 'He is so rich in kindness and grace that He purchased our freedom with the blood of His Son and forgave our sins.' - Ephesians 1:7.

2. **Cleanses us**: 'The blood of Jesus, His Son, cleanses us from all sin.' - 1 John 1:7.

3. **Justifies us**: 'We have been made right in God's sight by the blood of Christ.' - Romans 5:9.

4. **Sanctifies us**: 'To make His people holy by means of His own blood.'- Hebrews 13:12.

5. **Life / Communion (in relationship)**: 'For the life of the body is in its blood. I have given you the blood on the altar to purify you, making you right with the Lord it is the blood, given in exchange for a life, that makes purification possible.' - Leviticus 17:11 / 'So Jesus said again, 'I tell you the truth unless you eat the flesh of the Son of Man and drink his blood, you cannot have eternal life within you. But anyone who eats my flesh and drinks my blood has eternal life, and I will raise that person at the last day. For my flesh is true food, and my blood is true drink. Anyone who eats my flesh and drinks my

blood remains in me, and I in him. I live because of the living Father who sent me; in the same way, anyone who feeds on me will live because of me.' - John 6:53-57.

6. **Intercedes for us:** 'You have come to Jesus, the one who mediates the new covenant between God and people, and to the sprinkled blood, which speaks of forgiveness.' - Hebrews 12:24.

7. **Access for us:** 'And so, dear brothers and sisters, we can boldly enter heaven's Most Holy Place because of the blood of Jesus.' - Hebrews 10:19.

8. We are, therefore, in the right relationship and are in every way protected/covered/blessed/saved/forgiven/guilt-free with Father God through the blood of Jesus, His Son.

C. **Word of our testimony:** Our testimony is not only what the Lord has done for us, but also the testimony of the word of God in our life. When creation came into being, God spoke. When the stars instantly came into existence, God breathed, and the stars were born. God made creation (space/time) and set things in order. Our testimony is about proclaiming God's eternal and powerful word into our world. There is also inherent power in the words we speak too.

From the same tongue, we can speak health or harm, truth or lie, good or evil, building or tearing, help or hindrance, wisdom or foolishness, strength or weakness, hope or hopelessness, laughter or sadness, encouragement or discouragement, comfort or fear, and the list goes on.

With our words, we testify about what God has done in our lives and how we are transformed. We testify about how we are now forgiven, that we are in the right relationship with Him, and that He has a wonderful and personal plan for each of us. We speak the word of God in our testimony of His goodness and grace that is upon us.

D. **Declarations:** As mentioned, words are powerful and can change and transform our lives. They set the tone of how we live and do life. Declarations deem what is acceptable for living and what is not. Declarations are the foundation of how a society, principle, conviction, position or state of being is to be perpetuated. This is why It is so important to 'declare' the word of God over our own lives, the lives of those around us, and the situations and circumstances we are experiencing.

You and I are agents of change (and are His sons and daughters), and there is inherent power in the words we speak. Both words and actions can change the course of a life. That is why we must be careful with the words we put out into the atmosphere. Words invoke emotion and responses. They carry with them the capacity and ability to bring life or death. Words are one of the greatest tools in our personal armory. What you say today will either make or break somebody. They will either build you or demolish you. They will either liberate or imprison you. They will weaken or strengthen you. When you listen to music, why do you feel or think or react in a certain way? It's probably both the music and the words that affect you. Possibly taking you back to a moment in your history that you liked or that was dark for you. Either way, it is personal, powerful and deeply profound.

One of the main reasons why words are so powerful and moving is recognising the source of words. Words originated from an infinite Spirit, God. Everything God is and does is characteristic of His nature, essence and substance. I'll explain.

God is Spirit.

God is Love.

God is Holy.

God is Light.

God is Eternal.

God is Ever Present.

God is All-Knowing.

God is All Powerful.

God is a Consuming Fire.

God is a Father.

Another aspect to consider is that all humanity is made in the image of God. This means that you and I and every other person who has lived, who now lives, and who will live, are eternal beings. We are in a physical body with a soul and spirit. Human beings carry features of the creator God. We have all been hardwired with a sense of eternity: **'He has planted eternity in the human heart.'** - Ecclesiastes 3:11 When you and I speak, therein is the power to affect every person and situation for either good or bad.

So, regarding Authority and Power, there are two important realities to consider with the Word of God and how we do life.

1. **Authority**: To have the authority of God is to be in a position of privilege; we have been given the capacity, the ability, the right, competency and freedom, jurisdiction, delegated influence and force to take action in fulfilling His purposes in and through our life or into a situation. When God created man and woman, he gave them the position of authority and responsibility to tend the garden, and name all the animals and flora. Everything was under his (man's) dominion. But you see, Adam gave all that authority away when he and his wife sinned against God in the garden. It was only when Jesus came to earth as a man that Christ took back the authority the Devil had stolen. Consider what happens when we operate in the authority Jesus gives us: **'Look, I have given you authority over all the power of the enemy, and you can walk among snakes and scorpions and crush them. Nothing will injure/harm you.'** - Luke 10:19

As recipients of Jesus' authority, we must first know what that is; that we already had received it when we consciously received/accepted Jesus as Lord of our life; and that we also learn how to use this authority so we can effectively carry out His will and experience His freedom. You and I are also responsible for using His delegated authority in our lives. He gives us gifts and specific tasks to carry out to fulfillment. This is to establish and expand His domain.

2. **Power**: When you firsthand operate in the authority and power of God, you are authorised to speak out and release God's miraculous power into a particular situation. **His power backs your authority.** 'In the name of Jesus, be healed!' You have the right to speak and call on the name of Jesus, and it is with His power/ability/potency/effectiveness/ and might that He backs or validates that authority by working a miracle in the situation at hand.

E. **Renewing our mind:** Our mind is a combat zone. Daily we have skirmishes and scraps of contention. We are fighting ourselves or our incessant enemy, the Devil or at least his cronies. **'For we are not fighting against flesh-and-blood enemies, but against evil rulers and authorities of the unseen world, against mighty powers in this dark world, and against evil spirits in the heavenly places.'** - Ephesians 6:12 You see, the Devil wants to make us doubt God. And as a helmet protects our heads/minds, we must take on and secure God's word to protect our life and mind.

The Bible says that we have the mind of Christ, which means that we can think like Him and take on the things that are close to His heart. The renewing of our mind transforms us. Becoming more Christlike. We change the way we think through the word of God. If you want to know what God thinks about life, money, sin, work, people, purpose, adultery or any other matter, you will discover it in His word.

When we are transformed by His word, we demonstrate His word by how we conduct our life, even towards those who have hurt us. When we take control of our thoughts and what we allow in, we are taking charge. This is only possible by the renewing and transforming power of the living word.

Regarding our thoughts, we may not be able to control every external factor, but we can control internal factors. **'Bringing every thought into captivity to the obedience of Christ.'** - 2 Corinthians 10:5

This Scripture, in practice, might look something like this...

(Not a formula, only a suggestion)

- Refusing to entertain / not to keep thinking on the thought
- Take your position of authority and tell any tempting or deceiving or lying spirit to be silenced and to GO in Jesus' name
- You could then declare a relevant Scripture to have God's word take place and charge over / in place of that thought
- Give Father God praise and thanks for being part of your life and equipping you to be able to do this

This practice is not natural but supernatural. This ought to be common practice in the believer's life. Remember who our common enemy is and who our awesome Lord is. **'The Spirit who lives in you (the Spirit of God/Holy Spirit) is greater than the spirit who lives in the world.'**
- 1 John 4:4.

F. **Lining up / Agreeing with God's word:** There are a few considerations here. First, we must consider our words. Second, our response. Third, our faith and trust. An excellent example of this is Abraham. Stay with me on this.

Abraham obeyed God and did everything God purposed him to do. The Lord said go, and I will show the land to you. Abraham said yes. He didn't know where he was going, and even when he got to the land where God had led him, he camped there by faith. Abraham did not know the land where God was leading him to go, but he chose not to have unbelief (or even have a refusal to trust and obey God) in his thoughts, his heart or confession. He maintained his faith and trust, and we know this because he made it to the land God had appointed for him to inherit.

Abraham also trusted God in his actions by willingly giving up his son Isaac as a sacrifice to the Lord. The Lord did not want Abraham to kill his son; he was testing Abraham's faith. And he passed with flying colours. In fact Abraham was so close to killing his son that the angel had to call out to Abraham twice to stop him. This man chose to obey the Father and not to waver in his faith nor abandon his confession to negative or faithless speech. He honoured God with his words, his faith and his actions. And God honoured and blessed him for that. And you and I are no different.

G. **Prayer and Breakthrough: 'In everything, give thanks; for this is the will of God in Christ Jesus for you.'** - 1 Corinthians 5:18 As you know, not every situation or experience in life is positive or pleasant. So when you are experiencing a tough time, it is thanking and praising God through the situation that will help you navigate it. This is particularly difficult because this is 'naturally' the last thing you feel like doing. Worship (not just expressed as singing) and trusting in Father God is a spiritual act. Remember, though, that in this, He is with you. He enables you to overcome. He strengthens you to get through it. He can use you in the future because of it. He empowers you from it. He grows and develops you as a result of it.

Father will provide you with the physical and mental ability and capacity to enable you to make it through to tell the story. He will give you the means to guide you through the right course of action to take and the courage to do that job when that time comes.

He will promise to help you out of your situation/struggle and protect you. God always carries out what He promises to do. We must trust His timing on things. He is for you and not against you. He is on your side. Breakthrough happens at a critical moment. **It is a partnership of your faith and His faithfulness.**

Father God wants to bring you physical healing and mental/soul well-being. He understands how important you being at peace is instead of being in pieces. He can take away your anguish, pains and the sting of past events. What I personally know is that through process and time is that the presence and power of God is working within you; and that the power of your past cannot last.

That's why it pays to be specific with the questions for Him and to tell Him exactly how you feel about things. And to tell Him your thoughts. He sees how you cope with things and how you manage your heartaches. This is where Holy Spirit comes in. Years ago, I broke my right collar bone, it snapped like a twig, but over a couple of months, it knitted back together and healed strong. But from a young age, my damaged heart and soul did not mend quickly or even mend at all. The Lord has given us a body that can heal itself and become strong and resilient. That's our physical part. As for the non-physical aspects of our being, they're the parts that only God's Spirit can touch, reveal and heal.

That's why we can't do it alone and try to get spiritual results by physical means. When you become 'born again' by the Spirit of God, this is a two-person spiritual act with eternal outcomes. So, prayer (talking to God), waiting (trusting) on Him for answers and results, with faith (the confidence that what we hope for will happen).

CHAPTER 8: WHY ARE SOME DADS GOOD AND OTHERS BAD?

A dad that is seen to be bad might display ongoing behaviour such as: manipulating, controlling, abusive (mentally, physically or verbally), coercive, violent, short-tempered, absent, angry and scary, threatening, addicted to substances, neglecting, extreme mood swings, unpredictable, emotionally unstable, unsupportive, unloving, disengaged, mean, lacks communication, shows no interest in your life, treats your mother poorly, disrespectful, no boundaries, shows no compassion, heavy-handed, never says 'I love you,' harsh, negative, arrogant, discouraging, condescending, irresponsible. This list does go on, but you get it.

Another aspect apart from the expression of behaviours is the reality of having no sense of protection, security, provision, or feeling safe. There is no role model, structure in the home, or active/engaged parenting.

Comparatively, a dad that is seen to be good might display ongoing behaviour such as encouraging, supportive, loving, kind, understanding, saying 'I love you,' displays integrity, consistency, compassion, taking an interest in you, giving, discipline, caring, present, reliable, respectful, responsible, self-controlled, active in your life, treats your mother well, has boundaries, leads by example, engaged, patient, resilient, communicates, prioritises family. Again, the list goes on, but you get it.

So, it still leaves the question of why some dads are good, and others are bad. So, with no particular order, let's look at some examples. In addition, a good dad might instill a sense of wellbeing, is an active and engaged role model, providing a sense of safety, security and provision for their children.

Many factors show us why numbers of fathers are more on the front line, and others are not. Cultural reasons, for example, exhibit the mother playing a more prominent role, and aunties or uncles (because of their involvement) may also be called mum or dad, or cousins may be called brothers or sisters. It is their way of connecting and to their land, their identity. The father is not entirely out of the picture but raises a child differently than a dad might in western society.

Modelled behaviour is monumental in how a dad performs and how a child develops. A poor model will promote poor behaviour. Kids are watching all the time, and they take notes and mimic behaviours. If your dad did not have a positive or actively involved father and was not taught how to be a man or be a good father, then how can he do a good job himself? This may also be perpetuated in you as well, in varying degrees.

By the way, it is only my aim to provide you with some further understanding here, which will hopefully become an asset for you on your journey with your dad and (if you intend to do so) with your transition into fatherhood too. I am not trying to defend anyone or take sides but to promote thoughts to provide insight to make your journey easier and more practical for you. That said, my dad, as you know, was not around to show me anything. But I will share with you how his choices have affected me with my own family but also how God has been a father to me and the impact He has had on my life. More of that is to come in the second part of this book.

One of the practical steps which have helped me in my journey is not only letting go and forgiving, and subsequently moving on; it was to **gain an understanding** of why things were done in the first place.

Things like:

- Why did he leave?
- Why did he go away?
- How could he have been so irresponsible?
- Why did he not own his choices of marrying my mother and fathering his children?
- Why did he leave her in debt?
- Why did he skip town and not make any real effort over the years to communicate with me?
- How was he ok with starting another family thousands of kilometers away and neglecting the other?
- How could he be a bad dad on the one hand and simultaneously be a good dad on the other?

To give one response, let's first look at **humanity** then the **man**.

Humanity

Learning about the nature of human beings will go a long way in your journey, and mine for that matter. I believe getting insight will help us better understand why people do what they do and possibly even learn about what led to certain decisions and help shed some light on certain behaviours.

The nature of human beings

'Since we are made in God's image, we are intricately, delicately, ingeniously, fearfully and wonderfully made.' - Psalm 139:14. You and I are very complex beings. We have a physical body. We have our psyche, mental capacity, conscience, and soul. We have intellect, emotions and self-awareness. We also have a spirit. However, you look at a human being, we are eternal beings that are conscious of a higher being; God and I are endowed with intelligence, and awareness, and we live in a physical body that differentiates us from others. We are unique in so many ways; our DNA, our eyes, our fingerprints, our tongue prints, our personality, our desires and humour, and the way we see and do life. We have individual world views that may or may not align with others, but that's part of being a 'one-off.' Your disposition about issues and things that matter to you. Your own tastes in foods, music, personalities, clothes, job/career, circle of friends, personal beliefs, holiday destinations, the furniture you like, where you live, and the climate you want. And your sense of humour and personal convictions.

But regardless of how you look at things, **What matters to you, matters to God**. He made you on purpose for a purpose. And

He likes what He sees. And just like every single human being that has been, that is, and that will ever be, Father God cares about you and loves you for who and how you are. **You were designed for destiny.**

Despite all this being true, there is something I must include to give a fuller and more accurate picture of humanity as a whole. Originally human beings had a faultless nature. Then, one day, everything changed. Desire, the human condition, creation, destiny and relationship with God all decayed and have been problematic ever since. What am I talking about? The one and only – Sin.

So, what is sin, and what does it have to do with anything?

At first glance, sin is what you want with a total disregard for everything else. It is the most selfish state of being and condition of the self. It separates God and man and is evil. Sin is the absence of life, light, love and the Lord. The resultant decayed state of environment and ego is now separated from His holiness and health. The state of sin changed you. The absence of life and light leaves you in a state of darkness and death. Sin alters your mind, your attitudes, your health, your destiny, your life, your relationships and your essence; your very being is bent on self.

Sin distorts the original and turns things into twisted and tainted realities. The reality of the work of sin takes all hope and skews the truth. Sin is to miss the mark, fall short of God's Holy standard, and refuse to listen, obey, or follow Him. It is to dismiss His words and to follow after your own way. To sin is to consciously and purposely disobey God's words and commands.

There are many expressions and symptoms of sin, and the sin that goes unchecked is sin that will inevitably control you. You are a slave to that which controls you. Sin doesn't want accountability, either. Sin has no boundaries or stops, and the longer sin resides in you, the easier it is to do your own thing, and the less you feel or sense conviction by His Holy Spirit calling you and bringing you back to a place of repentance.

Every human being has been affected by sin its effects, and to varying degrees. We each have our struggles with this or that, and even when others seem to have all things together, they do not. No person alive is exempt from the effects or consequences of sin. Sin initially broke the bond between man and God. From the outset, it has been a fight for futures for every human being. Your future, my future, and our family's and friends' futures depend on the war we wage on sin and its effects. From the beginning, humanity has been infected by sin. This scenario almost seems hopeless to begin with.

But there is hope and help available to us. Not only do we struggle with personal issues we also fight against spiritual powers at work. **'We are human, but we don't wage war as humans do. We use God's mighty weapons, not worldly weapons.'** - 2 Corinthians 10:3-4a.

If you and I are strictly physical, why do we use spiritual powers or authority to fight against the problem of the day? Behind the veil of this physical reality lies the domain of the spirit dimension/realm/reality. Not all problems are solved equally. Different problems require alternative responses.

You see, over generations and time, people have been involved in many acts of sin. Many of the problems we see today result from past decisions, bloodlines and traditions. This natural realm is inextricably linked to the supernatural realm. And while not all supernatural ties are good or holy, that leaves the unholy and evil.

Believe it or not, when the first two humans, man and woman, made their mark on earth, they began to die, and we inherited their 'nature/state/condition'. Fear, guilt and shame were a few of the first symptoms of sin that appeared. Pride, disobedience, lying and blame-shifting were undoubtedly among the first expressions of sin that found themselves on the platform of the earth in the beginning. And they have been here ever since.

Humanity was broken and banished from the presence of God. And has been like this ever since. What a disaster. Thank God He sent a cure for this sickness of sin, and He is known to us as King/Lord/Saviour/Redeemer/Messiah – Jesus. He made a way when there was no other way back to Himself (God). Jesus brought us close to the Father when works could not. We could not earn our way to God, but we could learn our way to Him by hearing and responding to the voice of the Holy Spirit and repenting of our sins to be reconciled back to Him.

Throughout all Scripture, people were not healed, nor delivered, nor made well, nor forgiven, nor restored, nor blessed, nor purposed, nor guided, nor empowered, nor at peace without the power, presence and love of Almighty Father God. Human beings are in a hopeless place on their own. Now I could make a list of 'sins' that have troubled and tormented the human race since the beginning, but that would take too long. But here is a list that all people will relate to God's Holy Ten Commandments.

The propensity, susceptibility and effects of sin are deeply ingrained into every person's heart, mind and nature. It's no

PART 1: DADLESS...

surprise then we have the problems we face and endure today. Sin-natured people reproduce sin-natured people. But Jesus Christ breaks all the power of sin and curses upon his people if, by faith, we surrender to Him and repent and make Him our personal Lord and Saviour.

Do you see now how the nature of human beings has affected this world and how we all live in it? Sin is such an unholy thing, and it affects human behaviour and all things that are subjected to it. But thanks be to God; we now no longer have to live under sin or its power. It is His power that breaks the hold over our lives. There is now no longer any condemnation for those who are in Christ.

When mum and/or dad display broken/poor behaviour, often, the result is broken children who usually repeat the same behaviour to varying intensities and measures. But the same applies too with positive and good/better behaviour. Aspects of life are not always bad, but we live in a 'fallen' world. And the only way through it is with the Lord's presence in our lives.

The Man

When my dad left, he was very young. He was around nineteen or twenty years of age. Mum was slightly younger. So, this brings me to the first point.

Age / Maturity

He was quite young and clearly not ready or willing for the responsibility of life. Even though he married my mum, I would say that there was a lack of personal grit and maturity in taking on a family. The easier (not better) option was to jump ship.

It just wasn't his time. He was not intended or equipped to handle such a life-changing event. There would seem to be a lack of personal development and life experience/skills and understanding. He may have felt that he did not want to have the responsibility of having a family. There is also the aspect of not enjoying the life of feeling tied down and not being able to live his life the way he wanted.

Character

He probably didn't have the grit, inner strength or integrity to take on and carry the responsibilities that ensue with having a family. His upbringing may not have been ideal either. His dad probably didn't model what it takes to have a family and be a good dad. You cannot take someone where you have not been yourself. In other words, you cannot model what has not been modeled to you. **You can't give what you don't have**. His character may have been weak as his dad failed to instill into him the very thing that he required to see the bigger picture and stay the course.

Fear

Who does not experience fear at times? The thing with fear is that our thoughts, emotions, actions and decisions can be rash, rushed and reckless. Our behaviour can be out of character and even extreme. And the outcomes and effects can be permanent. We are emotional beings, and fear is one emotion that can (if we allow it) alter our thought processes, change behaviour and limit/distort our perspective of a situation. When fear is present, that is not the best time to make big and important decisions.

Circumstances

I know when my dad was young, he worked on the railway. But I am also aware that there were debts as well when he left. So, whether he was working at the time just before he left, I am not sure; however, there seemed to be problems financially. I cannot be sure whether this was a money management issue, lack of work, or a measure of both. But whichever the case, the situation would have it that there was a lack of providing and security for us at that time. Could he not handle the stresses and pressure at those crucial times? I may never know for sure, but I suspect this may have been in the mix of things.

Self-worth

It is possible that when my dad looked at himself, he saw a man he didn't want his sons to become. Many dads out there see themselves as not worthy as an individual and also being a dad. They have very low self-esteem, and their personal value or estimation of themselves is low/worthless at best. And they may compare themselves with others also. And sadly, when we do this as human beings, we almost always see ourselves as lower or less than those to whom we are comparing ourselves to.

These false and inaccurate views may have come from other people we grew up with telling us we were useless, bad, we were nothing and no one loves or cares for us; these lies and discouragements are then taken as 'truth' into our thoughts and personal beliefs. As far as Father God is concerned, we are created equal in His image.

'So God created human beings in His image.' - Genesis 1:27. And, Christ died for <u>all</u> humanity. **'He died for everyone.'** - 2 Corinthians 5:15.

The amazing thing Christ did for all of humanity is He put everyone on a level playing field. He died for all, and gave everyone the same opportunity to receive Him, to have a future and hope, to have healing, to have favour in and upon their life, and to know Him personally.

No role model

Though people usually have an innate moral sense of right and wrong, good and bad/evil, how can you or I model a 'good' example if we have never received firsthand those lessons ourselves? It isn't easy. But not impossible. I am not excusing anyone's behaviour or what they have done or are doing, but I do put forward the question: 'How can my dad give me or provide me with good examples of behaviours if he didn't get those lessons himself? This is more a change of perspective than a charge of blame. This may not change his ways, but this helps me to consider my ways.

Lack of love

Love is the greatest thing we could ever give or receive. So, when you don't experience it, you begin to wonder why not. Was it my fault? What did I do wrong? There is something wrong with me; It must be me. What a field of lies to walk through!

Other people make their choices. All my life, I had assumed that my dad loved my mum, at least, but was this true? To be honest, I don't know one way or the other. And the same goes for us three boys also. Did he love us? All I know for sure are the circumstantial events. We were abandoned, but by God's love and grace and mum's hard work, we got through. I would expect through all this that my dad possibly carried a load of regret with him.

But God, in His goodness, has also provided my dad an opportunity to heal from his hurts and receive forgiveness. But I have reached a point in my life that it is better to let go of what I didn't have and embrace what I do have. My physical dad, in a sense, showed me how not to be a father, and my spiritual dad, the Lord, showed me how to be a father.

So, being that there would be other reasons as to why on his part, he was a bad dad, he also started a new family and was deemed (by his new family) as being a good dad; How could this be?

I think what helped me with this is that human beings have the capacity/ability to be either good or evil, moral or immoral, ethical or unethical, honest or dishonest, loving or unloving, etc. Even though I cannot give firm answers to this question, I can only surmise at best.

Although my mum and my brothers did not get what a dad ought to provide, at least his other children and wife received a better experience. It's positive to state that he didn't make the same mistake twice, for their sake, at least.

CHAPTER 9: THE DADLESS EFFECT ON CHILDREN

The potential impact of absent fathers can be significant. Depending on your demographic, the effects and issues will differ. For example:

PART 1: DADLESS...

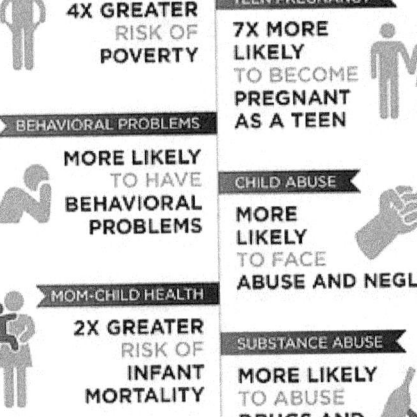

https://www.fatherhood.org/father-absence-statistic

As you can see, this information is American-sourced; however, the effects are similar wherever you look. In Australia, the UK, Canada, Europe, Asia, the Middle East, wherever your roots are, the effect of an absent father has had a significant impact on you. Conversely, if you take each of these points and take a present father approach, the opposite would be profoundly different. So, we change the statements of 'More likely' to 'Less Likely.'

Mothers give life; fathers perpetuate it.

CHAPTER 10: SO WHERE TO FROM HERE?

Before I finish the first part of this book, I want to summarise a few things.

1. The effect of absent fathers and the influence of fathers that are present are either life-shaping or life-changing. Not having a dad or a good dad usually has a negative impact, whereas a present, though not perfect, dad has a more positive influence. I know this is obvious, but when you consider how your life has been shaped by past events and you are trying to form a new future, you're in the middle, and sometimes you get stuck or fed up. When you look back over your life and weigh up the good and bad aspects of your father, I want to encourage you to persevere, and be committed to the change you want to achieve. You may have a long way to go, but the effort and continuity of transformation will bring out your worst and instill the best God has for you.

2. Here is a short activity to do. You may want to be a dad as a younger or older guy. Even if this is not on your wish list, you may find some practical steps here that will benefit you. Whichever the case, I would like for you to make a list of the things you do like about your dad; or a list of things about another dad you know and have

observed. Then make a list of things you don't like about your dad. Lastly, make a list of the things you don't like about yourself and then finally, a list of things you do like about yourself. There will be four lists in all.

Make this list now or whenever you can. But do this soon. You and others will benefit.

1. Your/Others' dad (Like)
2. Your/Others' dad (Don't like)
3. Yourself (Like)
4. Yourself (Don't like)

Each of these lists should include things like skills, character traits, behaviours, attitudes, etc.

Now, this is the point. There are a couple of things happening here. First, you will see things you don't want in your life from these lists, so cross those out. Now, you will also notice items on the list of things you want in your life. So, focus on and practice those good and influential things. They will benefit you, your family, your friends, and others who are part of your life.

Ask yourself; What kind of man/father do I want to be? In time you will begin to see the good fruit of your work.

5. From this activity, you want to declare (through prayer, personal declaration, and by your actions) that your father's negative/poor example will not be duplicated or repeated in or through you and how you live your life. You want to stop the cycle handed from father to son/daughter and begin a new legacy that will one day be handed down to your children.

PART 2: ...BUT NOT FATHERLESS

CHAPTER 11: GOD IS FATHER

Let's get straight to it. For human beings to better know God and to begin to understand who He is, His nature and His character, in addition to going to Him, we must also go to His word, the Bible. This will help you to gain more insight and to be able to better relate to Him as He wants to be closer to you personally as well.

When we look at the word 'Father' in the Bible, both old and new testaments, we know the words to literally mean - Father. **Nowhere** in Scripture does the Bible ever say, mention, infer or imply God as Father-Mother. Apart from other characteristics and His magnificent nature, God is a Father. He is the father of Jesus.

'This is My beloved Son, in whom I am well pleased.' - Matthew 3:17.

'Our Father who is heaven...' - Matthew 6:9.

It is also interesting that in the Muslim faith when referring to 'Allah,' there is no reference to him as being 'Father.' However, there are at least ninety-nine terms that describe him. But these are merely terms that tell of what he is like or what he does, but no personal term for connection between him and man (humanity). Any 'relationship' that there may be is also based on works, not faith. So, one must earn their reward, but that is not even guaranteed when going into the afterlife.

PART 2: ...BUT NOT FATHERLESS

In humanity's limited and finite understanding of the mysteries of God, I want to mention the concept and reality of the Trinity. I don't want to get off the main track too far here, but this subject is one briefly worth mentioning here in that it's relevant to the overall content of this book. As best as I can, let me give you this analogy to help describe the trinity.

First of all, though, I will say that the word 'Trinity' is not actually written in the Bible, but the concept/reality of it is. You see, God the Father, God the Son and God the Holy Spirit are separate beings but one in nature, in substance. They are the same in essence but different persons in positions, authority, and location. God is on His throne. Jesus is seated at the right hand of the Father, and the Holy Spirit is in every believer who receives Him. Please excuse the oversimplification.

When Jesus was on the earth, the Holy Spirit was in heaven, and after Jesus ascended to heaven, He sent the Holy Spirit to come and reside in every believer that would receive Him, to be empowered by Him. I am removing the complexity of things, but I am only presenting you with the tip of the iceberg of infinite truth and reality. I will finish with this analogy.

The Trinity is like a door hinge. The hinge is made of three separate parts but of the same material. They are bonded or joined together by a central pin that makes them complete and one. They are perfectly one, and simultaneously maintain their distinct, separate roles, function and being. The three parts are one hinge. Or the hinge comprises three distinct unified components.

My aim here is to distinguish each person from the 'Godhead.'

CHAPTER 12: GOD IS A FATHER TO THE FATHERLESS

From a Scriptural perspective, what does it mean to be fatherless?

Going from the Hebrew word 'fatherless,' we get a sense of being lonely, a bereaved person. A fatherless child, an orphan. - STRONG'S CONCORDANCE - Heb. 3490.

When we look at the word 'bereaved,' we get the sense of being 'deprived...through a profound absence.' Other synonyms include words such as: robbed, stripped, orphaned, sorrowful and grieving. Have you ever felt any of these emotions? I know I have. It's tough to be on the fatherless side of the fence.

But it goes further. With another Hebrew word for 'fatherless,' we learn that from the primary root of the word, we get the meaning of to be nothing or not exist, be gone, never, no (where), without. In a negative sense - incurable. - STRONG'S CONCORDANCE - Heb. 369.

Connected with this is the sense of query (depending on usage) - Where?. From these accurate and descriptive words, it is no wonder we start to see and feel for ourselves how profound and devastating the effects of being without a father have upon us. When a father is non-existent, gone, absent, withdrawn from our life, the reality of a sick, grieving, sorrowful, incurable, stripped, deprived, the angry and lonely heart is often what is left behind. Our hearts are fully aware of the emptiness it contains because of an absence or abuse of a father, and so our minds and lives are full of tears and fears that compound over the years from those events. In reality, we're quite bruised and broken.

In God's plan, though, we were never meant to be fatherless. It was never intended for anyone to go without. To be fatherless is painful at times, and if gone unchecked and not dealt with, the effects can be severe. Living with the adverse effects and issues can be a direct result of not having the presence of a father in your life and not dealing with those matters of the heart and mind head-on.

There is also the fact that dealing with certain issues, as said previously, is also a matter of the Holy Spirit to manage. Being fatherless can suck at times, but it is not a life sentence, nor need be a detriment to your health, wellbeing and future. That's why in order for God to be a father to you, He requires you to be His child. You and I and every other human being that receives Him into their lives is a child of God.

CHAPTER 13: WHAT DOES IT MEAN TO BE PART OF GOD'S FAMILY?

This is an amazing privilege and blessing. We were lost as orphans, but now we are in a family.

Adopted

We are placed as sons/daughters of God. You and I are positioned and are under God's responsibility. We are now in His care. **'The Spirit Himself bears witness with our spirit that we are children of God.'** - Romans 8:16.

When a child is adopted, there is a legal process that takes place; it's not a simple handover. Before you and I are God's children, we live under the wages of sin, which is: death, and separation from God with no mercy. When we become His children, through faith in Jesus, we are new creations in Him, and we no longer live under the penalty of death, but we now have life. Our eternal and spiritual status has changed.

By the blood of Jesus, we now have access to the Father. We are not slaves of sin anymore but heirs of God through Christ. God, the eternal Spirit, is not just a powerful being but has come down to us through the person of Jesus Christ, His Son, our Lord, and co-heir, and we can now freely and confidently call

God our father. We are born again at the point of repentance and God, who is Spirit, legally becomes our father, and we are now in His family. We are now sons and daughters. Your new birth certificate from heaven, the Lamb's Book of Life, is now inscribed with your name.

Recognition and Privilege

We now have rights and privileges because we have a new birthright as God's children. We have the right to be called sons and daughters of God through Christ, and we are also eligible for an inheritance from Him.

'And because you are sons, God has sent forth the Spirit of His Son into your hearts, crying out, 'Abba, Father!' Therefore, you are no longer a slave but a son, and if a son, then an heir of God through Christ.' - Galatians 4:6-7.

Personal Responsibilities

We are to do life with the life-changing power and guidance of His word - Romans chapter 6, for example.

'Well then, should we keep on sinning so that God can show us more and more of his wonderful grace? 2 Of course not! Since we have died to sin, how can we continue to live in it? 3 Or have you forgotten that when we were joined with Christ Jesus in baptism, we joined him in his death? 4 For we died and were buried with Christ by baptism. And just as Christ was raised from the dead by the glorious power of the Father, now we also may live new lives. 5 Since we have been united with him in his death, we will also be raised to life as

he was. 6 We know that our old sinful selves were crucified with Christ so that sin might lose its power in our lives. We are no longer slaves to sin. 7 For when we died with Christ, we were set free from the power of sin. 8 And since we died with Christ, we know we will also live with him. 9 We are sure of this because Christ was raised from the dead, and he will never die again. Death no longer has any power over him. 10 When he died, he died once to break the power of sin. But now that he lives, he lives for the glory of God. 11 So you also should consider yourselves to be dead to the power of sin and alive to God through Christ Jesus. 12 Do not let sin control the way you live; do not give in to sinful desires. 13 Do not let any part of your body become an instrument of evil to serve sin. Instead, give yourselves completely to God, for you were dead, but now you have new life. So use your whole body as an instrument to do what is right for the glory of God. 14 Sin is no longer your master, for you no longer live under the requirements of the law. Instead, you live under the freedom of God's grace.

15 Well then, since God's grace has set us free from the law, does that mean we can go on sinning? Of course not! 16 Don't you realize that you become the slave of whatever you choose to obey? You can be a slave to sin, which leads to death, or you can choose to obey God, which leads to righteous living. 17 Thank God! Once, you were slaves of sin, but now you wholeheartedly obey this teaching we have given you. 18 Now you are free from your slavery to sin, and you have become slaves to righteous living.

19 Because of the weakness of your human nature, I am using the illustration of slavery to help you understand all this. Previously, you let yourselves be slaves to impurity and lawlessness, which led ever deeper into sin. Now you must

give yourselves to be slaves to righteous living so that you will become holy. 20 When you were slaves to sin, you were free from the obligation to do right. 21 And what was the result? You are now ashamed of the things you used to do, things that end in eternal doom. 22 But now you are free from the power of sin and have become slaves of God. Now you do those things that lead to holiness and result in eternal life. 23 For the wages of sin is death, but the free gift of God is eternal life through Christ Jesus our Lord.'

Living life as a follower of Jesus is not perfect on our part, but He enables us to make better choices, think like Him, speak differently, change our hearts and see the world and people around us through His eyes. I will stress the pressure is not to live 'perfectly' but humbly, open and obedient to Him.

Walking in the Spirit

When we walk in the Spirit, we live in a strength and power, not our own. God is Spirit and we have Him residing within our being/spirit that changes everything. You and I have created beings that have limited and finite abilities. The Holy Spirit, however, does not have these limitations. The only stopper, though, is when we are not in line with His will; this then caps what He can do in and through us. So, what does it mean to live/walk in the Spirit?

Let's first look at the fruits of walking (living) for ourselves and then living (walking) in/with Him.

'**19 When you follow the desires of your sinful nature, the results are very clear: sexual immorality, impurity, lustful pleasures. 20 idolatry, sorcery, hostility, quarreling, jealousy, outbursts**

of anger, selfish ambition, dissension, division. 21 envy, drunkenness, wild parties, and other sins like these. (Let me tell you again, as I have before, that anyone living that sort of life will not inherit the Kingdom of God.) **22 But the Holy Spirit produces this kind of fruit in our lives: love, joy, peace, patience, kindness, goodness, faithfulness. 23 Gentleness, and self-control.** There is no law against these things! **24 Those who belong to Christ Jesus have nailed the passions and desires of their sinful nature to his cross and crucified them there. 25 Since we are living by the Spirit, let us follow the Spirit's leading in every part of our lives. 26 Let us not become conceited, or provoke one another, or be jealous of one another.'** - Galatians 5:19-26.

It becomes clear then that when we decide to exclude the Lord in our everyday life, we can go off track far and fast. But when you and I make a heartfelt choice to live for Him and to trust Him and to go on and stay on His path for us, the two paths are distinctly obvious, which is more beneficial in this life and in eternity to come? It is easier to go and live for ourselves. It takes more grit and resolves to live supernaturally rather than just naturally.

To walk or live in the Spirit is to be in step, to be preoccupied with the Holy Spirit and to be about His business. It's like walking in deep snow and stepping into the deep impressions that follow Him, stepping where He has led. It is seeking after Him and waiting for Him to further guide and lead you to what's next. Is it always straightforward? Not all the time. Do we always know what's up ahead? No. Will we always have the answers? No. But this is true in life anyhow. Living a life by faith is not living blindly. It is a lifestyle of trust, hearing from Him, and having that peace that settles in our spirit and soul and moving forward from that point.

When you are about Kingdom living, you are operating in Kingdom authority and when breakthroughs, answers to prayer, miracles and healings are taking place in front of you, in a sense, this is not out of the ordinary for Kingdom standards. This is the standard of His Kingdom being displayed in your sphere of influence. King Jesus came to establish His kingdom, His standards, His authority, power and reign. You and I are His children, serving Him and bringing about His domain.

Being Holy

Being holy is to be set apart and dedicated to the Lord. To be a sacred thing. To be clean morally. To be pure or blameless or figuratively innocent. **'Pursue peace with all *people*, and holiness, without which no one will see the Lord.'** - Hebrews 12:14. It would be **living to God's standards in our human state, with the help of the Holy Spirit**. When you separate yourself from the Lord, you are deciding not to live attached to this world. You live in this world, and have a connection with it, but you are not its property; you do not belong to this world; you belong to the Father. In the world but not of it. Holiness is seen in the fruitfulness of your life.

Righteousness happens when you first come to know the Lord by the blood of Jesus. Holiness is the evidence of a life pleasing to God. We get a pretty good picture of what it means to live pleasing God. It's not always easy to live a holy life, resisting temptation, and avoiding potentially life-derailing moments. But with His strength, we can overcome and make it through with flying colours. Remember that He will always make a way out of those critical situations.

Being holy is not just about you or me either. It is also about those who know us and observe us. It is for their benefit as well. How we live our life can inspire, encourage and motivate others to do likewise. When we stop and take inventory of how we conduct ourselves, what attitudes come out in situations, what we do in private as well as in public, the words we say, the behaviour we display all play a part in how we honour the Lord, ourselves and to those around us. We are not the ones perfecting ourselves, though there are things we can do to improve, the Holy Spirit in us is doing work to complete us, mature us, perfect us, enhance us and make us more Christlike. We are individuals and unique in every way, and the Lord would have us live as our unique selves, the way He made us, for we are His workmanship, made in His image for good works at this very time.

We are favoured/blessed

When we are living a pleasing life to God, we have His favour and blessing. God won't bless or turn a blind eye to sinful living and disobedience. But as we live for Him and seek His will and endeavour to run our own race of faith, through giftings, desires He has planted within our heart, our dream or personal vision in the context of His will and purposes for you, God not only empowers and enables us, He also equips us with the means to accomplish His will.

Throughout the Old Testament, we see numerous accounts where people are subject either to judgment or blessing when it comes to living for themselves or living for God. It's pretty obvious how to live to experience His goodness and blessing. It is vital to where in your heart/life you place God. If He is not central and foremost, what is before Him? If God is second place in your life, clear the way and make room for Him to be first.

We are blessed because of what Christ has done for us already. We are made righteous because of His sacrifice. We are shown mercy despite our sins. We are saved and forgiven by His blood that He willingly gave up for us. God graces us with His kindness and goodness – a blessing and favour. The fact that you are alive today is evidence that God chose to be merciful and gracious to you (and every other human being, for that matter).

But there is our part to play in all this too. When God makes a promise to us, we are to respond with faith and obedience. We are to seek after Him and have a grateful heart and response to His word. Jesus tells us in Matthew 7:7-11; to ask, seek and knock. Being active in Godly activity is vital in hearing, receiving and experiencing the favour and blessings of God. So, these two things come in the form of supernatural and natural expressions. There are both the physical and spiritual out workings of His goodness.

Being In His Plan

For eternity, God has had the plan to love and be loved by His children, human beings. The family unit as we know it is the building block and core structure and constitution of community and society. It is this close relational environment where people can love and be loved, have guidance and safety in life, and grow and develop in social settings and treat and respect other human beings.

As the founder of Youth With a Mission (Lauren Cunningham) once said, it is to 'know God and make Him known.' God is all about family. And while the effects of sin in this world are not always in line with God's plan, He provides us with His grace, love, mercy, kindness, goodness and care to experience this and express this with others. According to His blueprint and design. Being in the family of God also provides us with identity, learning/having a sense of boundaries and limits for healthy lives and interactions with others. Being a family member has its purpose and place of belonging. Being in God's family, first and foremost, means that God is our father, and we are His children. This means that through Jesus, we can have a direct relationship, access, and communication with Father God. We also have a greater family to get to know, and the reality of eternity to look forward to.

When God is your inheritance, your cup of blessing is full. What I mean is that even in this life and eternity to come, your present and future are taken care of and secure. Though life may present some problematic and dire circumstances, He is faithful to help us and get us through. Being in the family of God has many benefits. We have an identity; we have a purpose, we have a larger family and belonging, we are not alone, we are predestined for great things, and we have access and privilege to a higher power.

Now we can sometimes think that because we have screwed up too many times (or so we believe), it is too late, or we are now out of the race of life and what is the point. Or there is no hope or reason to continue; no one on this earth is beyond the reach or grace of Jesus. His sacrifice, blood and resurrection took away the world's sins and you are no exception to this truth.

'I can never escape from your Spirit! I can never get away from your presence! 8 If I go up to heaven, you are there; if I go down to the grave, you are there. 9 If I ride the wings of the morning, if I dwell by the farthest oceans, 10 even there, your hand will guide me, and your strength will support me. 11 I could ask the darkness to hide me and the light around me to become night 12, but even in darkness, I cannot hide from you. To you, the night shines as bright as day. Darkness and light are the same to you.' - Psalm 139:7-12.

Every human being lost the privilege of being in a close relationship with the Father when our ancestors, Adam and Eve, went their way and screwed it up for everyone. If it were not for love and Son of God, we'd all be lost and separated from God forever. We were all once disqualified from coming to God, but by His grace, we can now finally make amends and be at peace with Him. God loves us despite our sins. He first loved us. He loves us not for what we do or how successful we are in life; He loves us because He loves us. And we bring Him great joy. We are the apple of His eye and precious in His sight: no catch, no strings and no conditions. Just love. Love is all-powerful.

'If anyone loves Me, he will keep My word; and My (Jesus) Father will love him, and We will come to him and make Our home with him.' - John 14:23.

Some last thoughts are that we have knowledge about God that gives us strength and confidence through life. We know that He is with us; he knows our needs even before we become aware of them. He will never leave nor forsake or abandon us. He will provide for us and protect us.

Father God also understands us and counsels us with His Holy Spirit. He knows what is best for us. Thank goodness He doesn't always answer my prayers how I want. That would be disastrous.

God has our lives mapped out for us, without being disrespectful. Father God is our One Stop Life Shop, and our life membership is paid in full by Jesus. Thank You, Lord.

CHAPTER 14: HOW IS GOD A FATHER TO ME?

This part of my life is my entire walk with the Lord. I want to take you on the path that I am on, and I trust my personal experiences will benefit and strengthen you on your life journey. I will take you from day one to this present day on how God has been a father to me.

He First Loved / Chose Me

Even before I knew God, Jesus and the Holy Spirit; He knew me, and they first loved me. My journey as a believer and follower of Jesus started when I was about 15 years old. My family had no particular 'religious' or 'spiritual' background, so the whole 'God' thing wasn't a part of my life. But it was no coincidence that I grew up in a small town in Australia at this point in history. Even the friends I made and hung out with were by no means accidental either.

I had one friend in particular who was involved with a church where we would go and learn about the book of Revelation once a week. The information I was listening to was exciting, and it just seemed to make sense to me. The guy leading the seminar was an ex-Hells Angels member who used to 'take care of business' on some issues. I thought, man, he's a good guy; if God could get a hold of him and turn his life around, God must be real.

Around that time, there was a new family that had moved into town, and their two girls went to the same High School I went to. Being a small town, we all got to know each other and became good friends. After a while, their mum and dad began to have a weekly study group. They would have a video, a talk, some prayer and almost definitely food afterward (the best part, of course). As best as I can recall, after so long, the dad of the house said to me, 'Do you want to ask Jesus to come into your life?' I said, 'Yeah, ok.' In essence, I simply remember that I repeated a prayer after him, parrot fashion.

What I experienced was simply unforgettable; nothing at all. There was no thunder and lightning, no spiritual experience, no supernatural event that I could remember. And that was that. But what I realised after the fact was that in all that time, I had been going to those seminars for Revelation series, coming to the house meetings and watching and listening; my faith had grown. God got me; He was so sneaky!

I didn't really understand what was happening over the course of around 12 months, but He was doing a work of faith in me, and I never saw it. Nothing in all that time and since has been an accident or random event. God always had a plan and predestined me to be in the right place at the right time, surrounded by the right people. Ever since I met with God, He has become even more real to me over time through my personal relationship with Him.

You see, God draws us to Himself by His goodness and kindness, and it is by these that He leads us toward repentance.

If God never loved me in the first place, I would certainly not be around sharing my story with you now. He would not have set the whole scenario up of me being in a place where I could get to know Him personally. If love doesn't cost you anything, then is it really love? But God, in His unconditional love for this world, for you, for me, sacrificed His Son. This is love.

'We love Him because He first loved us.' - 1 John 4:19. Father God had shown me His love towards me through others by giving me what God had given to them; love and acceptance. **I never knew what a Father's love was like until I met God**. I didn't have to do anything, be special or be successful. He accepted me for who I was with unconditional, no strings attached. He reached out to me through other people He had touched. He did this in such a gentle and uncoercive way. And He desires to do the same to you and, through you, for others.

Also, **'But God showed His great love for us by sending Christ to die for us while we were still sinners.'** - Romans 5:8.

The truth of the matter is: **'You didn't choose Me. I chose you. I appointed you...'** - John 15:16.

'For God saved us and called us to live a holy life. He did this, not because we deserved it, but because that was His plan from before the beginning of time – to show us His grace through Christ Jesus.' 2 Tim 1:9.

We may have had faith and asked Him to come into our lives and forgive us for everything we have done; we even received Jesus into our life, but He did all the groundwork before anything ever existed. He foreknew us all, and we responded to His call; It's called repentance.

His Timing Is Perfect

Since God knows everything and He is perfect in all His ways, it was for my sake that He came into my life at the age I was. As I understand, the vast majority of people come to know Jesus at around the age of 15 years. So being in that category, I am thankful since I could have gone on a very different path if He hadn't intervened at that point in my life. Every person has a timeline in which we are all headed in the same direction in terms of eternity; a dark, lonely and torturous eternity.

However, when God intervenes in our timeline, our life and destiny alter course, and our future is changed for His good will and our sake. Only God has all knowledge and foresight, so He knows that at any other moment in our life, if He were to intervene and present an opportunity for us to repent and follow Him, we may not be ready, or it might be too late, or it may not happen at all. Then tragically, we would be lost forever.

'When we were utterly helpless, Christ came at just the right time...' - Romans 5:6. (This is referring to when Christ came to earth to do His Father's will for the entire world. But I have referenced this verse to make a point of His perfect timing in His overall plan for each person). King David said: **'My times are in Your hand.'** - Psalm 31:15.

Our lives are in His hands, under His control. God came into my life at the perfect time for me, and people and circumstances were shifted at the right time in my mid-teenage years. If the timing was later, I may have passed up opportunities and gone on a course that could have made me blind, and my heart turned hard to the gentle prompting and presence of the Holy Spirit working in and around my life at that time. I trust in His timing. And His timing for you is just right too. Because He knows you better than you know yourself. He knows all your future decisions, desires and inclinations and the very things up ahead that may distract you and unknowingly derail you from a destiny with Him.

He Protects Me

This is a present tense statement, an ongoing gesture of His unconditional love. And for you, too, for that matter. Let me first start with a biblical example of His protection. This will lay a platform for my experience. The account is where Paul and Silas (Acts 16:6-8) traveled through the present-day Republic of Turkey. They were explicitly instructed not to go to a midwestern province then called Asia. Then they were both intent on going to a more northern province, previously known as Bithynia. But again, the Holy Spirit had prevented them from going there, also. So, they ended up bypassing those two provinces and headed over to the west coast to the seaport town of Troas. There was no specified reason why the Holy Spirit had prevented them from going to those areas; maybe God had other people in mind to go there instead. In any case, they maintained the course the Lord had set before them and were in His will and plan to do great things.

I have often found myself being led by the Holy Spirit to avoid certain areas or roads to travel on. Even choosing which travel agents to go with. Going back some years, my now wife and I were about to get married, and we had to decide which agent to pay to handle the airfares to bring her family over from Sri Lanka to come to Australia to live. We were going to sponsor them. At that time, there was civil fighting in Sri Lanka and much unrest between the Tamil Tigers and the Sri Lankan Singhalese people/government.

My future sister-in-law and her two children were staying in a building in Colombo with the front windows shattered from a bomb that had exploded close by. We had agreed to sponsor them to come over but had to choose quickly who would be able to help them get out of the country legally and quickly. We were told to go with a guy suggested to us by a cousin over in Sri Lanka, but I remember it was at night, and Carmel, my then fiancé, was standing out in the front yard of my future mother in-laws' and we prayed about the situation. We needed an answer immediately. We initially thought that the guy referred to us was maybe the right person for the job, and it was the cheapest way to go as well. But at the same time, I remember this so clearly, we both looked at each other and said, 'No, this is not the right guy.' We both independently felt unrest in our spirits. He was not the right person for us to go with.

We then looked at other options and found the right person to handle the flights and other requirements for them to come over. We didn't know at the time, but it turned out later that we learned that the original guy suggested to us was somewhat of a scammer. We were guided by the Holy Spirit, and the peace that he put in our hearts set us on the right course.

Let me give you another example.

Years ago, I moved to Melbourne city, about a four-hour drive from my hometown of Albury. I moved to Melbourne for full-time study, and from time to time, I would make the trip back home for a weekend to see family and friends. I clearly remember one trip in particular as I was driving up to Albury; I had this impression or urge to just pray. I didn't know what I was to pray about but I just had this sense of urgency to pray and keep praying until I sensed/felt it was time to stop. So off I go, driving and praying in the car. I prayed in English and the gift of the Holy Spirit; tongues. And yes, it is an amazing gift, and I highly encourage you to speak this gift of the Holy Spirit! Often! It is not a thing of the Devil, as some would believe or say. The Bible is quite clear about the source and purpose of this gift. Ok, so as I was praying along the road after about two hours, I felt that I had reached the amount intended, and it was time to stop. What needed to be prayed for was prayed for. I would soon learn that that prayer was for me.

I came to a short stretch of the straight road doing the speed limit of 100 kilometers per hour. I saw a white station wagon coming from the opposite direction. The oncoming vehicle came into my lane and headed straight for my car. We were both in the same lane approaching each other at approximately 200 kilometers per hour. There was literally about a second in which I had to react to the situation. I quickly swerved off the road (A big no-no, especially at those speeds where there is gravel at the side of the road) onto the side, missing all the guideposts, not losing traction or control, and just missing the car that sped past me. I somehow quickly got back onto the road and looked into my rearview mirror and saw the car that had scarcely missed me collide with the car directly behind me.

There was a loud explosion sound, and debris was all over the road. I immediately turned around and parked off to the side of the road near the car which was just hit. The Toyota Ute was on its roof, and the passenger side was completely crushed in. The driver was still inside. I rushed to him, checked for injuries and ensured he was ok. He had some glass in his arm, but overall, he was ok. I pulled him out of the vehicle and waited with him until help arrived. His dog was thrown out of the back of the vehicle and could not be seen. The other driver had more severe injuries, but thankfully, there were no fatalities.

There was no coincidence that the Spirit of God had impressed upon me hours beforehand to pray into the heavenly realm and declare the perfect will of God to happen. The situation could have ended differently if I hadn't responded to His call. I didn't need to know the details but just to trust in Him and follow His lead. Angels had been commissioned and were present with me that afternoon. And I know that those two other drivers were also spared.

'His faithful promises are your armour and protection...For He will order His angels to protect you wherever you go.' - Psalm 91:4, 11 **When God prompts you, you be prompt with Him.**

My Character Development / He is Gracious

I remember when I was 18-19 years of age when I got involved in a relationship with a girl at church that I knew was not healthy or good for me to be in. I'm sure that I spent about 12 months or so caught up in that relationship, and it just wasn't healthy for either of us. But God did work things for the good, and I will value what He did for me and to me in that time for the rest of my life. Two main things took place during that time that helped shape not only my character but His grace upon me as well.

Character

I'm not exactly sure when during this time in my life I had this experience, but I recall seeing my senior Pastor every week

PART 2: ...BUT NOT FATHERLESS

regarding issues I was dealing with. The prominent one was concerning my newfound 'friendship' with this church girl. To give you some context and honesty, the relationship was quite physical and not at all blessed by the Lord or my close friends. Though they remained my good close friends, I was by no means getting anyone's blessing about me going out with this girl. They let me work through it till I had the sense and the strength to get out of it. But they were always there for me.

As time went on and I began to get to know my senior pastor quite well, we were able to have some real conversations and honest times together. I remember telling him one day I said to him; 'You preach too long.' I'm not sure what brought that on or why I said that, but he reclined and said nothing for a brief moment and finally replied by saying, 'And you stuff around!' The atmosphere was tense for a brief moment, but do you know what the funny thing was? We both had a point to make, to a degree. LOL. After we got over the initial blow to our 'perfect' characters, we acknowledged that there was some room for personal tweaking. Not so much for his journey and transformation; but particularly for mine. My Pastor at that time, whom I respect so much still today, probably didn't need some young disobedient, inexperienced youth to critique his experience and abilities. But I took it upon myself to 'school' him – what a silly and naive move that was. But hindsight is a good teacher. And thankfully, he still cared enough for me to walk me through that time and take me through what I needed, which has led me to how I am today. He helped forge my character.

In one of our sessions, all he asked me at the beginning was, 'So, how was your week?' He reclined in his chair with a smile, arms behind his head, relaxing. I was sitting opposite him, almost dying because I had to tell him how my week went. I replied; (And I was referring to my relationship with the girl at church), 'Well, we didn't do anything; I only touched her boob.' He then responded, 'I bet you thought you were going alright.' To that, I said, 'Yeah.'

But what he asked me next was for me, the bombshell of my life up until that point. He asked a question that has stuck with me and helped forge and strengthen my character. And I have never forgotten it. He asked me:

'When will you start being a man of your word?'

I was taken aback. Gobsmacked. I just sat there listening to him, caringly admonishing me and encouraging me, forging me into being a man of mettle. I will never forget that moment and the words he spoke to me. But also, the responsibility and character that he instilled in me at that moment and various times after that. God utilised men millennia ago to write His word, and still today, many people carry out His will, purpose, and plan. He uses His word and people to speak to us to build and bolster our faith and character.

'As iron sharpens iron, so a friend sharpens a friend.' - Proverbs 27:17.

He Is Gracious

It was also during this time that I had another couple from the church come along who cared about my spiritual walk and development and my personal wellbeing. Now in these situations, one could look at this and have the attitude of; staying out of my business and mind your own, and don't meddle where you're not welcome. But my position was that;

PART 2: ...BUT NOT FATHERLESS

I wouldn't mind some help as I didn't have the strength of character to make things right with all concerned. I felt weak about breaking things off, and I felt a little trapped. I didn't want to be in this relationship anyhow. I certainly didn't look for it, it came my way, and in hindsight, the better and right thing to do initially was to say, 'No thanks,' and walk away. So, I was about 18-19 at the time, and even though I was a young man, I was still a boy growing up in many respects. So, this couple from the church invited this girl and me to their place for dinner one night. We knew we were going to hang out and have a good time, but it was really to chat about our relationship.

Now, we had known this couple from church for a good amount of time, and he was one of the senior leaders there. His wife was also involved in a leadership role. They had our permission to speak into our lives. So, I was asked by Barry, 'Do you love her?' I said, 'yeah,' but deep down I know I didn't. I guess I had some kind of fear of expressing how I really felt. She had also said she loved me at that table as well. But I am pretty sure that Barry and his wife could see through the thin veil of truth and so wanted to present us with an opportunity to make things right for everyone wisely and straightforwardly.

So, after some further talk and questions, Barry and Lee brought a suggestion to the table. If the 'love' we felt for each other was genuine, would we be willing to step back from the relationship for three months to test the genuineness, authenticity, and strength of the relationship, and after three months, we would meet again? If we still both felt the same way and wanted to proceed with the relationship, then we would know if it was real love. So that suggestion made sense and sounded good to us. Probably more so for me than for her. However, we both agreed not to see each other for three months and not meet up by ourselves in that time. We could, of course, talk to each other at church. But no private meetings. I can see how this might come across to you as controlling or even quite harsh or unreasonable. But we each decided to be accountable to our leaders and committed to the Lord in honouring Him. How can you know if a relationship is genuine if it is not tested? This is just like faith. **Tested faith is Real faith**.

About a month and a half later, I spoke with Barry about meeting up again to discuss things. We got together, sat around the table, and with some facilitation from Barry and his wife, I then said to Elizabeth (the 'girlfriend'), 'With this time apart, I've realised that I don't love you. I'm sorry. I don't want to take this relationship any further.' It was undoubtedly a bombshell for her, but ultimately it was the best thing for both of us. Even though there were emotions to work through for both of us, for the short term, that is far better than having a life of regret and ruin down the track. But the good thing out of all this was that even though I had made a mistake on my part, God had graciously guided this wonderful couple from church and facilitated things so well that it was a win-win outcome for all. If you are in a relationship and are struggling to find a way out or wanting to end things amicably or with far less pain or any other negative outcome, consider getting some wise counsel and accountability. This may shorten the process and be easier for all concerned.

The lesson for me here was about how I see God and how he dealt with me through this entire process. Ever since, I have seen God firsthand display how much He cares not only for my eternal salvation and destiny but also for my earthly time and relationships here. God is love and wants us to experience His love and to show and extend that to others. But without His grace, none of this would have been possible. God is gracious in how He deals with us; by His grace through faith, we come into the right relationship with Him.

How Father has handled me over the years has been very gracious. He didn't let me off the hook. He didn't let me get away with anything. He taught me lessons. He humbled me. He also taught me through the lessons of others. He allowed me to grow and develop from others' experiences so I could avoid unnecessary heartache and pain. I was no more special than anyone else because God has no favourites. But He came across to me as a gentle but loving father. Gentle and loving do not mean soft or weak. He was not harsh nor cold towards me even after all the nonsense I went through and that He endured. But you know what? He went through all that nonsense with me. I have never sensed God being distant from me in my life. Ever! But even when I felt distant from Him at times, it was I that had moved. But even if you move, be quick about moving back under His cover.

He Guides Me

It was back in 2003 when I first started to think about getting some formal learning and recognised training with Bible ministry. Over the years, I had learnt and experienced a lot, but I wanted to get some sort of structured and official level of education and practice. So, I began thinking about the possibility of Bible school/college. About twelve months later, I applied to Harvest Bible College down in Melbourne. I started my course in July 2004, completed a Diploma in Christian Ministry, and graduated at the end of 2008.

But before leaving my hometown and moving to the big smoke, there were several confirmations and answers to prayer.

Desire

One remarkable aspect about everyone being an individual is that everyone has their own plan, dream, vision, gift, skill set, desire, drive, ambition, aspiration, idea, intention or heart to do or achieve something in their life. And it is unique for everyone.

What do you dream about? What do you want to achieve in your life? What things do you want to make happen? How do you want to impact your world? How do you want to add value to others? In what way do you want to help others succeed?

One way in which God guides us is through desire. God plants good things in the heart of every person, and He desires even more than us to see those plans and purposes come to pass with fruitfulness. Let me break down a few verses for you.

Psalm 37:3, 4, 5, 7. - **'Trust in the Lord and do good. Then you will live safely in the land and prosper. Take delight in the Lord, and He will give you your heart's desires. Commit everything you do to the Lord. Trust Him, and He will help you. Be still in the presence of the Lord, and wait patiently for Him to act.'** Let's take a look at these verses more closely.

These verses talk about having a confident trust in the Lord and by faith seeking, listening and acting out of obedience to him. Doing what Jesus did, doing good works, doing what the Father does and serving others. When we make time for God and expect to hear from Him, He communicates with us. There was a mighty windstorm when Elijah was on the mountain, followed by an earthquake. After that, there was a fire, but God was not in any of those. The text says, **'And after the fire, there was the sound of a gentle whisper.'** - 1 Kings 19:12. The Lord is telling you that when you speak to Him, He is near. The Lord spoke to Elijah in a gentle and quiet way because He was so close that Elijah could only hear Him because Father was close to him. So mighty, so excellent in power is God that God bent down and was right beside Elijah. And He is right here with you too.

So, when you begin to experience God's presence and atmosphere, you connect on a personal and powerful level. When you are transformed by the power and presence of the Father, you want to please Him. Lord, whatever You want. We then begin to realise that the desires in our hearts are the words and will of the Father He has placed upon us, and they agree with each other. So, we tell the Lord what is on our heart and begin to see His hand and favour working on our behalf. We cannot force or coerce the hand of the Lord, but when we are in agreement with Him, and we are in that right place, we are **positioned for promises**.

As we commit His will in our heart, He will help us accomplish those works of faith. Waiting with confident hope and expectation is what pleases Him. And when we please Him, there is the favour; there is the blessing and provision and peace that are inherent with being in His will. We influence our natural reach. We have power beyond our natural ability. We have authority beyond our natural dominion. We have blessings beyond our natural attainment. We have access to opportunities beyond our natural doors. The waiting is part of the supernatural process of His kingdom progressing in our lives and into this world.

In your own experience, can you determine your desires and what God desires for you, which ones He wants you to have? If you are having trouble or are unsure, that's ok.

Let's look at the meaning of 'desires' according to the word of God. Desires are requests being made into prayers and petitions. You inquire of the Lord and ask Him. There are aspirations, things that are, at least for now, out of your reach but are in God's reach for Him to be able to give them to you. I think that the hard part is not so much the part of getting those desires (aside from what it takes to get them; faith, patience, effort, sacrifice, etc..) but more the journey it takes to discern or realise which ones he wants us to have. This may come from the struggle between what we want and what He wants.

It's ok to have desires, but even better to have the ones he wants for us. I am so thankful He says no at times. I am grateful that He says to wait at times. It may simply be a matter of character and timing with some desires. Let me stress here; it is good to want things or to do certain things. Even though not everything we do, think, or want is good for us or will have positive benefits or outcomes for our life. So, we must ask God to help us see and discern those beneficial, helpful, purposeful, fruitful, and faith-filled desires.

The good thing about having desires is that they move us to get things done. They achieve and promote outcomes. They motivate you to take action, focus and get results. You want to see and make things happen. Father God desires us to be saved, healthy, fruitful, blessed, achieving and living fulfilled, meaningful and accomplished lives. Desire also means that we put ourselves aside, so we don't get in the way of serving Him. It's a life call to serve the Lord, but the relationship and rewards are infinitely bigger.

Let's pray:

Lord, help me to see Your will for my life and enable me to know what your plans and purposes are for me. I ask You to show me clearly which desires are Yours and which are not. I also ask You for guidance and wisdom in deciding my future plans. Show me which desires agree and line up with Your word and which desires do not. Show me from Your word, through prophetic words, Your peace, situations, or any other means you want to communicate with me. Thank You for listening to me, and I know that You will answer my heart's desire to love and please You. In Jesus' mighty name, Amen.

The fact that you have prayed this prayer tells a lot about where you are at regarding pleasing Him and doing His will. You're doing great; keep going.

So, to get back to the point of how God guided me. God had planted in me a seed of desire to learn more about Him, and that took on the form of attending the setting of Bible college. Not only was there a growing yearning or longing to do this, but there was also a determination to achieve this.

Desire is like a plant. You plant a seed, put it into good soil, water it, and wait. After a while, you see a green leaf, and to help things along, you give it some 'food' to nourish it and see it grow and thrive. After some more time with care and nurture, you see fruit. But you must wait for the right time to pick and eat it. Too early, the fruit will be sour. Too late, the fruit will be rotten. There will only be a brief window of time to get the best quality fruit.

Prayer

In a book about the late Billy Graham, he said the one thing he felt he didn't do enough of, namely, prayer. Though prayer was a significant part of his life, he did realise the power therein and how critical prayer was in daily life. Jesus often went off to pray on His own. If you are unsure what to do, prayer is the key. Conversation with Father is the answer. Jesus said it all the time; 'When you pray...'. The apostle Paul said, 'Pray without ceasing.' We are to pray in the language we understand and in the language of the Holy Spirit. Lots! Everyday!

When you talk to the Lord, you communicate and connect with Him. Prayer is not a magical formula or religious script but is in essence a devoted and personal time with Father. If you endeavour to do ministry without prayer, you ask for trouble. You would be going to war with a gun but without ammunition. Or he is going into battle without armour, protection or a strategy.

The book of Jeremiah 29 says that when you pray, God listens, and if you look for Him wholeheartedly, you will find Him. Psalm 34:4 says: **'I prayed to the Lord, and He answered me. He freed me from all my fears.'**

As we pray to God, that is part of our service. Through prayer, we find solutions to issues or problems we are facing. We also learn to trust God and have confident hope in Him through this practice. Prayer also helps us to keep in step with Him and to help us see life through His eyes. It provides an opportunity to have access to Him and for Him to tell us stuff. Finally, prayer shows us our need for Him. I get them when I pray to the Lord and need guidance and answers.

Wise Counsel

When I enquired about potentially leaving my comfortable surroundings and friends, I spoke to my pastor about my future prospect of moving away and studying full-time. We sat down, and my pastor asked me why I wanted to do this. Though I don't remember the exact words in the conversations that took place, the overall sentiment was to make sure that this is what God wanted, and, from his experience, he gave me other pertinent considerations to think about too. I recall that my aspiration to do this was growing more and more as time went on. I was also in a position financially, and being a single guy at the time, it was easier for me to make such a big decision as I was the only one to consider. I was responsible only for myself.

You only have to look at any high-level leader like a president, prime minister, or CEO and notice that they are surrounded by people who have others advising them on various matters and recommending courses of action to assess and proceed with. **'Without wise leadership, a nation falls; there is safety in having many advisers.'** - Proverbs 11:14. **'Plans go wrong for lack of advice; many advisers bring success.'** - Proverbs 15:22. **'When the Spirit of truth comes, He will guide you into all truth. He will not speak on His own but will tell you what He has heard. He will tell you about the future.'** - John 16:13-14.

But the biggest 'thing' I had to pray about and seek counsel on was whether or not I should marry this awesome chick I had come to know well throughout four and a half years living in Melbourne completing my course. But that all turned out just fine.

Some background: When I came to Melbourne, I knew no one except my former pastor and his wife, who had been working at the college I had enrolled in. Otherwise, I was entirely on my own and a stranger to these parts. Over the course of the next few months, I was looking for a church but didn't find one that was fitting for me. This experience on its own presented me with new insights and a firsthand understanding of various church cultures.

I visited about a dozen churches over 3-4 months. These churches and congregations ranged from being very solemn to being very youthful, inviting to being very stuck in an era, being very serious to being very joyous, being warm to being extremely cold and not even giving any eye contact, at all. Near the end of this church hunting season, I began to feel like I was running out of church options as I had exhausted all the nearby churches I wanted to potentially make my new home.

My method in finding my new church home, apart from asking my share-house mates where I should go, was using a city reference guide called Melways. This provided me with maps, directions, lists of businesses/organisations etc. I found this quite helpful in getting around and in finding my new home church. Before I left for Melbourne, my mum's fiancé had given this reference guide to me, as he was in transport at the time, and often would make frequent runs down to Melbourne from Albury. He would circle all his pick-up and delivery points and depot yards with a pen for quicker reference when driving in and around the city.

So, as I used this Melways to reference and mark my home and other locations, I would turn to the next few pages to look for churches as close as possible to go to each week. After some months had passed and I began to feel a little discouraged; I was looking at my home location and turned one page; right smack bang in the middle of the page, I saw where my mums' fiancé had circled one of his pickup points. I had never seen this one before, and it was one of the pages that I had looked at so many times over the previous few months. Right in the centre of the marked area was the name of the church I would, after, make my home for the next 14 and a half years.

I felt a sense of being at home even from the first visit. After visiting this new church a few times, I realised, yep, I have found my new church family, and I was welcomed warmly and sincerely. And since I had been involved with the music team back up in Albury, I was given an opportunity to be part of the team at Monash Christian Church.

Father God was really good to me in that the associate pastor at that time, Ps. Eugene welcomed me in, made me feel part of the gang, and just accepted me. He was such a cool and magnetic guy. A joy to be around and was always encouraging.

In looking for a church, I was also looking for a particular type of leader that I wanted to be my leading/senior pastor. After going from church to church, I listened to many preachers, and though good, I didn't find anyone that 'fit my criteria.' When I finally got to Monash Christian Church (MCC), I saw and listened to the senior pastor, Ps. Phil Martin.

Ps. Phil was a hands-on, in-the-trenches man's man. He was no-nonsense, but graciously pastoral and supportive. Phil didn't pull any punches, and his leadership, manliness, physical strength, and strength of character were solid. When I heard him preach for the first time, I think I had already decided that I wanted him to be my pastor. I was drawn to his character, leadership style, practical, simple, effective, efficient, get-the-job-done type personality, and pastoring.

Ps. Phil taught me over the years how to serve, to lead, deal with situations, how to treat and deal with people; he showed me both consciously and by how he did life and ministry, how to converse, how to counsel, how to develop character, how to be Christ-like, how to be a man of physical, emotional and spiritual strength. He showed me how to be a man and be a man of God. But sadly, a couple of years ago now, he passed away.

I know deep down that the very things I had been craving for in a dad, God gave to me in the person of Ps. Phil. I had fourteen and a half years with this great man, and I now have a heritage to hold on to and a legacy to live by and pass on to others. I think about him often.

Now that I had found my new church family, I, of course, got to know my now wife, Carmel, in the process. The shortened version is; after years of dealing with things and finally overcoming some issues in my life, I came to my senses and realised that Carmel was the one with whom I wanted to spend my life with. I think it was about two years that she liked me beyond just being a friend, but I was slow on the uptake. Over nearly four years, we had developed a strong and close friendship, an excellent basis for a relationship, by the way.

So, realising that I had feelings for her more than just friends, things came to the point where I needed to do something about it. I spoke to our senior pastors and explained how I felt. They were up to date, I think, on most of where we each were at anyhow; however, they suggested to me to go and spend a week praying about Carmel (I had already been in talks with the Lord about Carmel, but I was getting some good advice from my pastors too). Carmel and I were both independent at a point where we each needed to decide the other. Either we get together or forget the whole thing.

What I found out later really blew my mind as to what Carmel was praying about, but more what the Lord said to her during that time. And no one spoke to her about what I was doing. So, Carmel didn't know that I had spoken with the pastors, but God said to her in her prayer time, that 'This week, Brendon is preparing to decide for you.'

The following week after church, I asked to meet with her because I wanted to speak with her about 'something important. She knew what was going to happen. We went out afterward and told each other how we felt and what we each wanted and about things that were going on in each of us. It was so good to finally get it out, be on the same page, and enjoy being a couple.

But every step of the way, we each had counsel and accountability. At the time of this writing, it has been just over 14 years of marriage, and we have a 6-year-old son.

Situations / Providence

As I was preparing to wind up in Albury and give notice at work, with the apartment I was in, with the church and every other attachment there; I had to find a way to store my stuff for the entire term of study (at least two years). I couldn't take all my furniture and belongings with me, and there was a lot of stuff to store. I certainly couldn't afford to pay for storage either.

Out of the blue, a friend of mine had a business and a rather large warehouse with a mezzanine area with lots of space. He knew I was moving away and came up to me one day and freely offered to me to store all my stuff on his mezzanine in his warehouse. No charge, no strings and no problem. He just wanted to be obedient to the Lord and at the same time bless me and help me out of a potential 'rock and a hard place' situation. It was a timely and perfect answer to prayer.

Prophetic word / Word of Knowledge

While still living in Albury, It was in church one morning that we had a visiting speaker; and he had prophetic gifting which he was operating. Toward the end of the service, the speaker asked me to stand up, and he said to me point blank: 'You should be in full-time ministry; God wants you to go to Bible college.' It couldn't be any clearer than this. But if and when you get a 'word' from the Lord, let me run a few things by you so you can be sure if God is speaking to you and bringing confirmation.

- A. Has the word confirmed something you already know or want to do?
- B. Has this word reinforced what is already in your heart?
- C. Has this word been spoken to you previously by others?
- D. What does the word of God say about this? Does it agree/ is it in line?
- E. Do you have peace about it?
- F. What is the Holy Spirit saying to you?
- G. Ask yourself, 'Why' do I want to do this?
- H. Where does the Lord fit in with this word of prophecy?

I. Does this word/plan/desire/project/mission require faith?

J. Is there fear or faith at work within you?

His Word

Other than the Holy Spirit, there is only one other source that ought not to be substituted: the word of God. **'Your word is a lamp to guide my feet and a light for my path.'** - Psalm 119:105. So, when reading His word, we must always know what it is saying and read it in its proper context.

Ask the questions:

- What is this Scripture saying here?
- Who is it speaking to?
- What is the setting?
- What is the context?
- What observations do you have?
- How does this Scripture apply to my current situation?
- What can I learn from this?

We must also wait and let the Holy Spirit speak to us, helping us to understand the Scriptures. We must also consider what the word is and how we got it. When God spoke, He formed the universe, the stars, other galaxies and everything we observe and know. There is an order in the universe, but it is finite. The word of God was before anything ever existed.

After God formed man, He then breathed life into him; he became a living being. Jesus is the living word, and the Bible is the written word. There is life, power and action in the word, and when God handed it down, the man wrote what was given to him, and what we have today is the Bible. When God gave gifts to man, He gave His word on pages and in the flesh (Jesus the man).

Whenever I sit down to read the Bible, I seek the Lord to see where/ what He wants me to read. I usually have a plan as to where I am going to next, but sometimes I need a specific word, and I require specific Scripture. I then thank Him for the opportunity and privilege it is to have His word and that I can read it and grow from it. I then ask the Lord to reveal something new to me, a personal revelation, to give me deep understanding and insight. If you want to keep in step and remain in the right relationship with Father God, then the Bible guides us very clearly in how to do this. And to get and maintain power and victory over our common enemy, Satan. Jesus will guide us into all truth. The Holy Spirit will guide us into truth. The written word of God will guide us into truth. Other sources may not guide us to the truth.

The following books speak about and teach many things, but by and large Psalms will help you to speak/relate with God. Proverbs can help you to deal with people. Romans teaches us about human nature and sin and salvation. Hebrews talks about faith. From beginning to end, the entire word of God teaches humanity about our origins, purpose, and destiny. God's word gives us insights, wisdom, and knowledge about living with integrity and practical living, doing life better. It teaches us about who God is and how to get to know Him better. It gives us hope, confidence, peace, and strength, and we can relate to people who live by faith. We see how people struggled and overcame challenging situations. The Bible helps us to grow in character and be more Christ-like. It prepares us for what lies ahead and for eternity.

I remember one occasion when the Lord spoke to me (for my growth and good) about needing to step back from some friends for a while. I found this particularly hard because they were my mates, the only few people I hung out with. So, for about a year, I was intentional about not hanging out with them. I didn't understand why at first, but when the Lord spoke to me a year later, he said, 'Now you can go back to them.' And: 'You now have the strength of character you didn't have a year ago.'

1 Corinthians 15:33 says: **'Do not be deceived; bad companionship/company corrupts/ruins good morals/character.'**

This makes sense. God knew that my character was not strong enough to continue associating with my circle of friends; they would, and I would for that matter, compromise my integrity, character, and morals. God knew my weakness, and He knew that if I were to stay in that environment, it would get the better of me. I had to go and grow for a while. After that year, I somewhat lost interest in hanging out with them as I did, but we occasionally caught up from time to time. They told me that I had changed and used to be more fun. I took three things from that. First, they noticed that I had changed. Second, I had grown and changed for the better. Third, they had not changed at all. There was a growth development in my character and integrity. God wants you to win in life and not be in situations or environments that will hinder or harm you or cause you to fall and fail. In His knowledge and wisdom, He sets you up for success, not failure.

His Spirit

God is Spirit, and we are human beings. And we are made in His likeness and image. We are human beings existing in a physical body, with a soul and a spirit. We connect with God through His Son, Jesus. We have a relationship and intertwined closeness with His Spirit, the Holy Spirit. We invite Him in, and He comes to live within us. You and I are aware of God's presence through His Holy Spirit, the spirit of Christ within us. When we experience that inner peace, that settledness in our thoughts and heart, we have instinctual knowledge that not only is He with us, but He is for us and directing our life. **'The Lord directs the steps of the godly. He delights in every detail of their lives. Though they stumble, they will never fall, for the Lord holds them by the hand.'** - Psalm 37:23-24.

God reveals to us what we cannot understand. He shows us what we cannot see. He tells us what we cannot know. He gives us what we cannot attain. It is a desire for God to impart these things to His people that we ourselves cannot acquire. We wish we could do more in our own strength; however, if we were to live this way, would there be a need for Him in the first place? Faith pleases Him because He loves it when we depend on Him, and He wants to be there for us, and He just loves to bless us. We're His kids. Any loving parent just wants the best for their children and wants to see them do well and have a good life and for them to achieve and have a fulfilling life.

'For His Spirit joins with our spirit to affirm that we are God's children.' - Romans 8:16. Whether we realise it or not, God also/already speaks to us through our conscience. **'Even gentiles'** (non-Jewish people). This could also mean people who do not personally know God) **who do not have God's written law**

PART 2: ...BUT NOT FATHERLESS

show that they know His law when they instinctively obey it, even without having heard it. They demonstrate that God's law is written in their hearts, for their own conscience and thoughts either accuse them or tell them that they are doing right.' - Romans 2:14-16.

Every person alive knows that there is a right and wrong the fact that we instinctively 'know' there is a difference. For one action, thoughts or feelings of guilt, fear or shame may come. For another course of action, there might be a response of emotions of security, assuredness, or thoughts of being right or responsible. God's Holy Spirit also helps and reminds us of daily things. **'...The Holy Spirit, He will teach you everything and will remind you of everything I (Jesus) have told you.'** - John 14:16.

The Holy Spirit is awesome. He is the Spirit of truth and will let you know about your weaknesses and convict you of sin. He will show you what to do and how to get right with the Father and others. He enables you to hear from Him and get closer to Him, to also be fruitful and empowered to do His will and overcome struggles in our own life. He also intercedes for us, and when we pray in one of His gifts that He gives to us, tongues, we speak in His holy and perfect language, so God's perfect will is at work. He is at work daily in our life. But don't feel discouraged if and when you look at yourself, you think that you have not made much progress, that you should be at a certain point in your walk, or that you are not like others. Just keep allowing the Holy Spirit to continue working in and through you. And never play the comparison game.

When we compare ourselves to others, we will fall short; when we compare ourselves to Christ, we fall short. But God never called us to compare or compete with others. He calls us to help others. To help them on their journey. The Holy Spirit also gives us His wisdom, knowledge and understanding.

Another really cool thing that the Holy Spirit gives us is the Father's seal of approval. I am talking about the spiritual and legal seal, or mark or proof that we belong to Him. We have an authorised seal or signature upon us that declares we are His property, and we are in every way and wholly His. Jesus' own life was the ransom He alone gave for all of us to get us back and redeem us from the evil one. His blood sealed for us the contract or covenant for eternity.

'...God saves you. And when you believed in Christ, He identified you as His own by giving you the Holy Spirit, whom He promised long ago. The (Holy) Spirit is God's guarantee that He will give us the inheritance He promised and that He has purchased us to be His own people.' - Ephesians 1:13-14.

He Never Leaves Me

Early on in my walk with the Lord, it was when I was about 16 or 17 years old or about twelve to eighteen months into my journey. I started to go off track. I was hanging around people and doing things that were very distracting for me, and just took my attention and preference over God; for a time. There was around two months when I decided not to care about my relationship with God and just wanted to do my own things and have fun. At that time, one of my friends I spent a lot of time with got caught up in some unlawful pastimes and activities.

We would make our own gunpowder; we already had the proper fuse. So, we would make our own DIY bombs so we could go and blow things up. We nearly lost an entire school building once. One of the wooden walls had caught alight after putting one of our homemade explosives in a steel bin. Fortunately, the fire went out on another occasion where we had picked out a nice large, painted wooden letterbox of a random resident. This particular person's letterbox we had chosen seemed like a great way to test out our new 'product.' It just happened to be owned by an ex-military person who was in the artillery and said that the device we used to end his letterbox was good. He found his front letterbox latch on his back lawn, which had gone over the roof of his house that quiet, still night, some days later. He certainly wasn't happy with what we did; however, he didn't lay charges, and decided to see it from another perspective. He had every right to handle that situation quite differently, but he didn't. Talk about being gracious. The letterbox was quickly replaced.

So, over a brief period when I thought I knew better, I found myself getting into all kinds of stupid things and doing things that would see me potentially ending up on the road to ruin. I finally realised that I was making really bad decisions and being around people who didn't have my personal health, safety and interests at heart. I realised that I needed to get right with God again and be around people who were good for me.

But here's the point. I stepped away when I didn't want God around (This is bad), but He was there for me when I needed Him. He never imposed or forced Himself against me. But He lovingly and graciously allowed me to make my choices. Though I was not close to Him at that time (This was on me), He never abandoned me. Though I had stepped out from under His covering, He never actually left me. The truth is that wherever you turn, God will be there waiting for you to come back to Him.

'For God has said, 'I will never fail you. I will never abandon you.' - Hebrews 13:6.

This is true also when as human beings, we will struggle against the spirit in an internal fight that will be with us until we transition into eternity.

'15 I don't really understand myself, for I want to do what is right, but I don't do it. Instead, I do what I hate. 16 But if I know that what I am doing is wrong, this shows that I agree that the law is good. 17 So I am not the one doing wrong; it is sin living in me that does it. 18 And I know that nothing good lives in me, that is, in my sinful nature. I want to do what is right, but I can't. 19 I want to do what is good, but I don't. I don't want to do what is wrong, but I do it anyway. 20 But if I do what I don't want to do, I am not really the one doing wrong; it is sin living in me that does it. 21 I have discovered this principle of life—that when I want to do what is right, I inevitably do what is wrong.' - Romans 7:15-21

As long as we are in this human body, we will never be perfect. But it is only through the perfect saviour that we can be perfected, mature, and complete in Him, Like being refined like a precious metal through the refining fire. I thank God, not for my struggles but that I am growing through my struggles. And that He is with me in and through my struggles. When we are going through something, we really should ask ourselves questions. Instead of saying; 'God, get me out of this, we could ask the question; 'God, what can I get from this? What can I take from this?' And ask God to help you grow through your situation. **You cannot be refined if you do not go through the process. The process can be painful but fruitful.**

When the apostle Paul was preaching and ministering, there was an occasion when all those around him deserted him. All but Luke had left him. He says: **'At my first defense, no one stood with me, but all forsook me. May it not be charged against them. But the Lord stood with me and strengthened me.'** - 2 Timothy 4:16-17, God is faithful till the end. The fact that Psalm 48:14 states: **'He is our God forever and ever, and He will guide us until we die.'** is evidence that He can only guide us if He is present in our life.

His Goodness / Kindness

Goodness

1 Chronicle 16:34 says: **Oh, give thanks to the Lord, for He is good.'** To understand what it means to have God's goodness is to understand what it means that God is good. When the Bible says that God is good, it means many things like His essence, His nature, His character, His works, His will, His gestures, His actions, His gifts, His words, His works, His presence, His contributions to our lives, His ways, His benefits, His intrinsic substance, His appearance, His values, His morals, His very being, His intentions, His heart's desire, His plans, His creation, is good! Not only is 'good' descriptive of **who** He is, but also **what** He does.

If I can put it this way, God is good for our life. To have Him is beneficial for us. It is far better to have Him than not. It is for our sakes that He improves and enhances our life in every way. But God also benefits from having us too. He delights in us. He loves us. He shows us a favour. He adores us. He smiles over us. He sings over us. He goes out of His way to position us for His goodness and love.

God, in His goodness, gave us His Son and His salvation. It is His goodness that leads us to repentance. He allowed us to be in the right relationship with Him. Everything God is and all He does for us is for our good. When sin separated man from God, it presented us with an uncrossable gap, an infinite chasm between Himself and us. The only way the distance could be bridged was through His son's righteous act. God did a good thing for us when He made it possible for all humanity to have a relationship with Himself. This was by sacrifice and sanctification, and reconciliation. But before Jesus' time, lambs, bulls, goats and birds were used, but they were not enough to take away man's sins. God sent Jesus the perfect sacrifice to take our sins from us, bring us close to the Father, and bring us back into the right relationship with Him again (Reconciliation).

Over the years in my relationship with God, I have noticed that there is nothing I could have done for God to love me more. There was also no sin I had done that God would not forgive me for. The grace of God doesn't mean we have the right or reason to go off and do whatever we please. No. It means that whenever we do find ourselves caught up or involved in something short of His plan for us, we can confidently come to Him and repent of the error of our ways and know that He still loves us unconditionally and is waiting for us to come under His care and cover once again. It's God's will that none should perish. It breaks God's heart that He sees so many people today lost, lonely, enslaved to addiction, blinded to the truth, people hurt by well-meaning people that permanently burn bridges to relationships that otherwise could have been the bridge or gateway themselves for other people's salvation and healing.

Sadly, when church leaders or those who have a following make moral failures, they inevitably cause numerous others to derail their walk with God and to discourage and bring disillusionment to others who are at a critical point in their lives to turn away from God and everything He is about.

But that said, God, in His goodness, makes possible a way back for people to be restored, replanted, reconciled back to Himself, and in many instances, back into former relationships again. It would take too long for me to make example after example of my life as to God's goodness He has shown to me, but what I will say is for countless occasions where I have sinned, made mistakes, turned away from His goodness, made poor choices morally, turned down growth opportunities; Father has always looked at me, waiting for me to turn to Him and say sorry, and to then soak in His goodness once again.

I want to mention one last thought about God and His goodness. In your experience, have you ever found yourself saying, 'God is good.'? This might be from a situation where God came through for you or answered your prayer. It could have arisen from a job you got or that He brought you out of a stressful or tense situation. You may have even experienced the loss of someone close to you or witnessed an unfortunate accident. Is God still good? Did He show you His goodness in those experiences? How did you feel about God and His goodness then? How do you feel towards Him and His goodness now? I want to assure you that regardless of any event in history or your own life, '... **I am the Lord, and I do not change.**' - Malachi 3:6. Circumstances come and go and change all the time. There is no static timeline in life. Life is dynamic.

Effectively since the beginning of 2020, the whole world has changed. How we see life, how we do life, and how we engage and interact with others has significantly changed. Our personal and interpersonal lives are constantly being reshaped. And this can bring about a sense or feeling of uncertainty, apprehension, fear, anxiety, depression, isolation, doubt and even division. Conversely, there are times like these that can be the glue we need to bring us closer together. And this must be one of our highest agendas, as the Scriptures tell us that in the last days,' people will lose love for one another. Love overlooks a multitude of sins and keeps no record of wrongs. Love God, love others. Know God and make Him known.

God's goodness goes beyond our human comprehension and understanding. However, though we might not fully understand it, we can receive it. We certainly do not understand God, but He certainly understands us. He is fully aware that, as human beings, we fall and fail at times, and He graciously steps in and intervenes in our lives in ways that others simply cannot. Where we are unable, He is able. Where we cannot, He can. When we are weak, He is strong.

So, God is good irrespective of our situation, disposition or perspective. If we want to know Him more closely, we must trust Him even when conditions or situations are saying something else. Sometimes it's a matter of persistent patience and waiting on God to come through, handle the matter on our behalf, and see Him bring out the truth or resolve that situation. God is on your side; He has your back, and He wants the very best for you. We must choose to trust in His wisdom and ways since they are higher and far more complete than ours. If you think about it, it might be a good idea to list as many things and times when God has been good to you and then to thank Him for those. Let me give you a few things to consider. But make your own list because it is what He has done for you.

PART 2: ...BUT NOT FATHERLESS

When I...

...speak to Him. He listens to me.

...need direction. He guides me.

...need answers. He shows me.

...need assurance. He comforts me.

...feel weak. He strengthens me.

...am afraid. He gives me peace.

...doubt. He reminds me of truth and gives me faith.

...feel alone. He gives me His presence.

...sin. He forgives me.

...am open. He teaches me.

...am seeking Him, I find Him.

...am hurting. He heals me.

...am sick. He heals me.

...am unfaithful. He is faithful.

...need to learn. He corrects, disciplines, and teaches me.

...have nothing to give. He loves me.

...am focused on other things. He is thinking of me.

...come to Him. He is there for me.

...hope in Him. He never disappoints me.

...am stuck. He helps me.

...am feeling frustrated. He understands me.

...have needs. He provides for me.

This is just a short list of mine, but there are many things I am sure you will add to your list. This is God's goodness in action for you. He is there for you in every situation or needs you will ever have, for He is good.

His Kindness

So, what does the kindness of God look like?

Let me begin with some Scripture. **'4 But—When God our Savior revealed his kindness and love, 5 he saved us, not because of the righteous things we had done, but because of his mercy. He washed away our sins, giving us a new birth and new life through the Holy Spirit. 6 He generously poured out the Spirit upon us through Jesus Christ, our Savior. 7 Because of his grace, he made us right in his sight and gave us confidence that we will inherit eternal life.'** Titus 3:4-7.

We see here that the Lord's kindness has more than one element. First, he saved us. Not by our merits or works, but by what He did for us. He is merciful. He was not under any obligation to do anything for us; except judge us for our sins. He gave us a new life and start in Him by the Holy Spirit. Second, He was generous towards us. And it is because of His love towards us that we have opportunity and access now to Him through Jesus, unconditional access. Not only do we have life, but we have the assurance of these and other good things and favour.

When you look at the life of Jesus and how He responded and interacted with people, He loved them. To a person truly seeking Him and seeking repentance, and restoration, God will never turn them away. Lifestyle and background are irrelevant.

But not only will God accept us, but He also will never turn you away or from you. God's love and kindness for us far outweigh our sins and disobedience. Jesus is goodness and kindness personified. When you look at Jesus, you see God, His heart.

I often think about how this infinite being we know as God or Father; this eternal being of pure light, love, power, and holiness, is kind and compassionate. He is not evil, and no darkness is found in Him. He is perfect and beyond any or all comprehension. This supreme Spirit endears us and cares about our every tear and trouble. He doesn't get bored of us; He never wrongs us. But He only has good intentions towards us.

Whenever my young son comes running toward me with his arms up in the air and a smile on his face, I can't turn him away. My heart melts, and I want to hug him and tell him how much I love and care about him. If I am angry about something, I usually need time to settle, but because of my love for him, those emotions fade, and I find myself caught up in him again. But I discipline him when needed and teach and model to him (as best as I know) how to do things differently next time. God is kind to me when I screw up. God is kind to me when I have been willfully disobedient to Him. God has shown kindness to me when in my dark times He has given me His light through others to show me His support and love and to help me get through. And to learn to avoid those unnecessary dark times again. He has shown me kindness when I have rejected Him. And I cannot think of a time where He has abandoned me.

Amongst the many things my late pastor said and showed me was that in the believer's life, there is no other option when showing forgiveness toward others. Our instinct would dictate to us to fob them off and disrespect them or to just disregard them all together and then go to church or some other Christian gathering and put on the face of 'love' and pretend to be their brother in the Lord, which is another issue for another day. So, my pastor taught through example and firsthand situations that God has called us to integrity, forgiveness and reconciliation.

Reconciliation is just as important as forgiveness. I understand that reconciliation is not possible for all situations and relationships. Still, if it is a possibility, then this is part of the deal for all believers to exhibit and practice. **Forgiveness bridges the gap - Reconciliation closes the gap. Forgiveness paves the road for reconciliation to travel on**. You and I are reconciled/restored back into the right relationship with the Father by His Son, Jesus.

His Faithfulness

'If we confess our sins, He is faithful and just to forgive us our sins and to cleanse us from all unrighteousness.' 1 John 1:9.

God's faithfulness means He is Just, True, Sure, Faithful, Trustful and objectively Trustworthy. God is consistent with His character and nature. While God is perfectly justified to wipe out all humanity because of sin, this would be true of His righteous and perfect, and holy nature. But in His perfect love, He is gracious and merciful to human beings who have fallen short of His standards. So, God in His Holiness has the right to judge us and take us out, but God, with His faithfulness and being ideally just, or right in passing out judgment, means that He judges the sin and gives life to the sinner. All of the sin landed or was placed upon Jesus, and that sin was judged and dealt with when Jesus went to the cross. When Jesus rose on the third day, all human beings then and ever since have had the God-given opportunity to attain forgiveness of their sins and acquire eternal life through the resurrected King.

We are stripped of the guilt of sin and clothed with the blood of Christ. Redeemed. Innocent. Justified. Righteous. Loved. **God has the right to punish us, but we have the Son to pardon us**. The faithfulness of God is ongoing and more than just relating to forgiveness. God is faithful in finishing what He starts and constantly walking with us every step of the way through life. He is loyal to His word, which shows in our relationship with Him.

When I think of the simple yet true analogy of weekly rubbish collection, every week in their trucks, the garbage collectors come around, do their rounds, and pick up only the trash the people leave out for them to collect. If the bin is not out, neither is the garbage. And what happens is that quickly the amount of rubbish, and rotten garbage builds up, and now you can smell it at the other end of the house. After another week, especially during summer, the trash is reeking at an all-time high. It's a disgusting mess and getting more challenging to handle and deal with. Like clockwork, the drivers come by and take what they have been given to collect. And it is always easier and manageable with regular and consistent pickups.

Some residential areas have a hard waste collection service from their local council that happens maybe twice a year and is separate from the usual garbage collection. You arrange a booking, and they let you know when to put out the hard rubbish for collection at the appointed time. I remember doing this once, and I had the hard waste out for collection. As I was vacating the property, I had to get all the rubbish off the property so I could get my bond back. The problem was, there were a number of close-by neighbours that thought it would be a good idea to dump their rubbish on my front lawn as well.

After the contractors came by and picked up the rubbish, they left drums of oil and other items that were not allowed to be thrown out for collection. These were the items left by my fellow neighbours. Not the kind of things I wanted to go with. So now I have acquired other people's problems, which I had to deal with. Thanks, guys! Eventually, I got rid of the rubbish and received my bond in full. The point here is there is an expectation that every week on the same day, people come by to pick up what we have no further need of. But if we fail to do that one small task each week, things quickly build up and become a problem quickly.

The same is true for us. God faithfully comes into our lives and wants to pick up and take away all the stuff that we don't need in our life. Unfortunately, as human beings, we don't always pick up on the importance or understand that there are things in our life that can cause us to become, in a sense, sick or unhealthy. The sin-garbage and its effects on our life can become rampant and quickly. God knows that to be healthy people and on track with Him, we need regular spirit and soul cleaning. Continually going to Him in prayer. Repenting of any sin, we are struggling with and being accountable to others and being obedient to Him and reading His word and applying it to our personal life and situations/circumstances, listening, learning good teaching of the word, and being in regular and meaningful camaraderie with other growing and fruitful believers.

Keep short accounts with God. Being in step with His Holy Spirit. God is faithful in being there for us even when we are not there for Him. God never walked away from me when I did that to Him. He will never leave you nor forsake you either. But no matter what is in our life or how much junk is upon us or what it is that we are dealing with, Father God is waiting for us to respond to Him. **He can make us stable**.

Jesus hung on that cross for you, and me and what broke His heart was the fact that in the one and only moment in eternity, God looked away and forsook His only Son. God loved His son but turned away from the sin of the whole world upon Jesus. He was carrying our guilt on Himself before the Father. Our sin put Jesus on that cross that the Father could not bear to behold. And it was in that instant Jesus breathed His last and died. Thankfully on the third day, He rose from the dead and was crowned with power and glory. And because of this event, every person has the opportunity to be at peace with God and have eternal life through His Son, Jesus. **His peace is our pathway to life and freedom**.

He Disciplines / Teaches

I was probably in my early twenties, I had no vehicle, and needed to get to work or just to get around in general. Even though I was working, I was terrible with money. I was a good payer of bills but a terrible saver and money manager. I didn't manage money at all. I was never really taught or shown how to handle myself with money. I simply earnt slowly and spent quickly, with little regard for future consideration or backup. At this point, I had been a Christian for about 10 years.

By this stage, I had learnt that there were priorities and responsibilities that I was aware of but didn't really adhere to.

Not consistently, anyhow. On the one hand, managing money is an easy formula; spend less than you earn. Or less going out than what is coming in. Not living beyond your means. But living week to week is not always a stable or consistent event. Hours change, and jobs come and go. Work offers fall through; other people don't pay for your goods or services, unexpected expenses crop up, etc.

It's hard to get ahead or stay in front when things are seemingly stacked against you as there seems to be no way out of your situation. Life is not all laid out for us, but we can be prepared for unexpected events, so we are not blindsided. Or at least mitigate the effects of the occasion.

So, I was working in manufacturing at the time, and was getting a steady income. I went to church, and things were going along ok. But I didn't have my own ride. In my 'wisdom,' I applied for a bank loan for $10,000; I was planning to get myself a new motorcycle. After waiting a few days, the bank got back to me and rejected my loan application. I was quite annoyed, as I depended on this loan to get me out of my somewhat sticky situation. It just made life a little more difficult not having my own transport. Relying on others all the time for everything just sucked. Truth be told, when I had applied for the loan, I didn't even have enough money to make a local phone call from a public phone. I didn't have two coins to rub together, and I was expecting the bank to hand over $10k. What was I thinking? Not clearly, I know.

God wanted me to learn and live in the knowledge of His truth and goodness. Not my own delusion of wisdom and knowledge. But God taught me a lesson in discipline and obedience. Albeit, God, is gracious too. If I was to be a man of conviction, integrity, and solid character, I needed the work of His Spirit in my life to make better choices. And He knows just how to do that. It was around this time that I needed to grow in many areas of my life and faith, but for then, giving and being generous in obedience and wisdom was the lesson of the day. And even years later, I struggled with this most important area of Christian living and obedience to God. But over the years, I have consistently taken on and seen God come through many times with His blessing and favour with regard to being obedient to Him in this vital area. I was not taught, shown, or modeled regularly giving a particular portion of my earnings, or the reason why until Father stepped in and showed me the ropes.

You're really going to like what I have to say; this is going to help you dramatically. I needed not only obedience but discipline in my life overall. But in His wisdom, God knew that this was the most important lesson I needed to learn and live out at this particular time of my journey. And I would say that whatever you are going through now, keep on with it. Allow Father to continue working in you and through you. What He plants in you now will make for a great harvest of fruit in your life in the future. And those around you will benefit as well, regardless of His particular work for you.

Giving in faith is God's way of reminding you of what is truly His. When you do not give, God reminds you that the money you have is now open to the enemy and is now exposed for the taking. You no longer have any legal ownership or guardianship over the Lord's commodity you have in your possession. This is probably why you see money going out the window every paycheck, and are struggling. You see, God owns 100% of your money, and He only asks you to transfer a portion of it. Even though He owns 100% of the total anyhow, which he entrusts to you to handle and manage properly, He requires a smaller portion of what you have in your possession to trust Him with. Remember, it's not our money; it is all His in the first place.

When you say, 'It's all mine,'; then it will be harder for you to let go of it. When you take the perspective of; 'It's all His,'; then it is easier to redirect the flow of this commodity into the right channels and see God's hand upon it. Every time we do not trust God and take the money into our own hands, this exposes what we do have, and the enemy has a legal right to do whatever he pleases. He then steals it away in the form of every possible expense or unexpected event you could think of. There is no coverage or blessing or increase potential over that resource. If we are going to live the Good life, we must always live by faith and trust in him! Faith and money are two commodities that we cannot live without. And God desires we have more of both. But it does take commitment. We need to go from: I can't afford to give to; I can't afford not to give.

God always blesses faith and obedience. But He will never bless unbelief (the choice of refusing to trust and believe in Him), disobedience and choosing to live in fear. I get it. When things are lean, and you ask where the money is coming from to pay the upcoming bills, money for food, or cash to put petrol in the car or to pay the rent, we have to go to the point where we are actively deciding either to live in fear, rely on ourselves, or to live in faith and to rely on Him. It's a big deal; it takes faith, courage, perseverance, discipline, and support. But the rewards and peace are much more significant.

When you make decisions based on fear, this pushes out all hope of living by faith. Where we can clearly see that the money coming in is less than what has to go out, it is reasonable, in natural terms, to not give. It is not logical to give away chunks of our income which could be a deal breaker with food or rent, but God is Spirit, and He is supernatural. Therefore, it is irrational to not give when living in the supernatural. This is living in kingdom standards and under the care and cover of Father God. In addition, in the natural, we can look at where we can reduce our expenses and unnecessary outgoings.

To illustrate a point, Carmel and I paid off just over 50% of our home loan in eight years, and we had an $80k redraw facility on hand. But we never actually made a point to use that. However, on the one or two occasions we took from that facility, we immediately put back the amount we used. Our repayments were weekly (always pay weekly if you can, this will reduce the amount of interest you will pay over the life of your mortgage) and we always maintained paying slightly more per repayment than what was required. We also used our tax returns to help reduce the principal amount to reduce the calculated interest. Whenever we earned more than normal, we put extra on the loan amount where we could. Both my wife and I were working part-time jobs and have been low-income earners for several years, partly due to my health reasons. Also take into account that our private health insurance alone was over $4k per year. We both had made a decision to stay the course, and maintain that simple strategy. Approximately six months later (through the sale of our house, we were able to pay off the balance of our mortgage and purchase in full our current house we are now in).

So how did we manage this? It was reasonably straightforward for us. Carmel and I have this running joke where I am the CEO in our marriage and she is the CFO. She managed the finances. And this still works very well for us today. However, that's only part of the story. We reduced our outgoings where we could and utilised what we had and owned. I'm not trying to be a financial advisor here, but we can make practical decisions to help curb the costs of living. Always be on the lookout for new and affordable deals or other payment arrangements. See if your insurance or bank can give you a better deal. Can you tweak your membership options and rates? See where you can cut off unnecessary subscriptions/memberships. What are those non-negotiables and nice-to-haves? Do you need to change your phone plan to prepaid? How about those grocery bills? List your financial obligations, prioritise them, cut off the dead wood. Discern your wants and needs.

Truth is, our spiritual enemy can steal from us because sometimes we allow that to happen when we open the door for him to act. When we look at the story of the four soils, the Devil came and stole that which was planted in rocky ground. **The condition of the heart will determine the fruit of the harvest**. The fruitfulness in a person's life is proportional to the state of the person's heart. Remember, the money does not come from us; it goes through us. The Devil, or other demonic entities, take from us to steal away the potential of blessing and increase what God intends. When God has access and rights to it, He takes that and brings an increase and can grow it and causes it to be substantially more productive and effectual in its purpose. It takes faith, perseverance, discipline, and trust to see God breakthrough in this area for you and your family. And it is normal to feel stressed and fearful about this, humanly speaking. But it is not the norm according to kingdom standards. I have seen firsthand where God takes over our finances and ensures the enemy has no access or right to what is rightfully His/ours.

Remember, God wants to bless and increase you. Give Him the legal and fatherly right to perform a miracle for you and your situation. Give first what is His, and He will ensure that the rest of what is His, that which is in your possession, will be used more effectively and purposefully. Allow God the ongoing opportunities to come first and foremost in everything you do. Take God at His word. He can be trusted. Every time you give in faith and obedience, it is an opportunity for you to grow, see God come through for you, and bring increase and blessing into your life and situation. Each time we surrender our will to Father, there is a little more of Him that takes first place in our hearts and less of ourselves to compete for first place. **That which takes first place before God in your heart is an idol**. The good thing about all this is that giving allows you to see what is in your heart and how much of that thing fills your heart. It also tells you directly that whatever is competing with Father is the very thing you value or prioritise over Him.

Anything you place in front of God in your life and heart is really an obstacle before Him. The real test is what you do with the very things that the Holy Spirit nudges you, tells you to give up, surrender, put aside, do away with, and your response to that prompting or conviction He brings to your attention. Jesus spoke a lot about money; getting more money will magnify your true character and how important that is in your life. Let God be God in your life and maintain Him as the first place in everything that resides in your heart. Psalms 62:10 says: **'And if your wealth increases, don't make it the centre of your life.'**

I was not planning on saying anything about money or giving in this book, but it is relevant to everyone because we can't do too much without it. Also, money and the more we get will tell a story of our true character and integrity. Money is a means for purpose, not the master of our purpose. You will be enslaved to what controls you. I had to go through a process of discipline over time so that my character and faith matured to the point that God could trust me with more. Who or what will take first place in your life? I always ask Carmel, my wife: 'Have we given this month? Are we up to date?' She is always on to it anyhow. But I rest easy knowing that we are on track and squared away with this life-enhancing faith act.

If there is something God has taught me about Him over the years (apart from everything else); it is to know Him and remain in His will. The presence of God in and upon your life is what really matters. Let me share with you two brief thoughts about His presence in particular.

His Presence

His manifest presence

When you encounter the presence of God, it changes you. The tangible presence of God takes away all the theory and religious ritual, and ceremony. It puts on the reality of a real relationship and an atmosphere of love and peace. When I get into a time of prayer or to get time out, or I have to 'get it all out of my system,' I tell God everything. I cannot hide anything from Him, so I don't even bother. He knows it all, anyhow.

Although it is hard sometimes to get things out, I eventually get there. But whenever I sense or feel that God is near, He is close to me, just there, looking at me with the same kind of feelings and thoughts I have for my own son. Now I don't physically see God, but I know that He is close to me. I get a feeling of doting, care and deep love, and He just wants the best for me. He wants me to experience Him. He wants me to do well in every area of my life.

Have you ever experienced the presence of God? What was happening in your life when you had that experience?

I ask because some people have had a physical experience with God, while others have not. I mean that they may have had an angelic visitation, a vision, Jesus Himself has appeared to them, or some other fantastic experience. Although we can feel some physical effects of His presence, like peace, emotions, healing or deliverance, It is God's prerogative, and He acts in His goodness, grace and compassion. He knows perfectly what to give to each person. And whoever it is, He will always respond to faith.

But I do want to say something here: Keep tabs on where you point your focus, and whenever you go and spend time with Father, always have a thank-you list for Him, not just a shopping list for requests. Or that you are only chasing a physical encounter or experience. God will always meet you at your point of need, but in His wisdom, we have to take Him at that and know that if you have never had one of those encounters like others may have had, its ok. You don't need something like this to happen in your life for God to be 'more real' or for your faith to grow, feel more spiritual, or think that you deserve it.

Most probably, like me, you would like to have an amazing encounter with Father, but I am also of the position that if I live my life and have no meeting that I have sought after, I can live with that. For me, at least, it's the way to go. If the Lord decided to appear before you or bless you with some kind of spiritual encounter, that would be awesome, but remember, faith is key to how we live before Him. He does want to reveal Himself so much more to you, but how long would that experience last? I will also say that if He were to give us all the answers, as it were at once, our walk with Him would not require faith. Would there be a need to depend on Him if we had all the answers or the ability to handle everything ourselves?

God is not codependent, but He also knows that as human beings, we have many flaws, limitations and shortcomings that make it impossible for us to live completely successful lives without His power operating within us daily. Hence, we need the Holy Spirit to guide and provide all we need for successful living. My personal track record in succeeding in life is attributed to having the power and presence of God's Spirit living within me and for me to keep in step with Him. Yes, we do have gifts, abilities, skills and talents. Still, they are not enough to comprehensively understand and to have victory overpowers that are beyond our finite capacities that are constantly at work behind the thin veil of this reality and the spirit realm.

Whatever your current situation is, always be open and teachable to His Spirit. He has wisdom, knowledge, insight, understanding, foresight, perfection and power that we lack. That's where He comes in. Trust Him today.

His Continual Presence

Throughout the Bible God says He is with us, that He is near. He is only a prayer away. He waits for us to turn to Him, to trust Him. He is near enough that if He were to speak to us, He would only need to whisper in our ears. He is close enough to bail us out of trouble in our time of need. As earlier said, I have always felt or sensed that Father is near. I have never experienced Him far away or unreachable. Although sometimes I have thought that He was. I have felt at times throughout my walk with Him that I have gone through dry, arid and desert places, even for seemingly long periods. It just seemed like hard work and lots of effort to connect and commune with Him. I haven't felt this way for a long time, but looking back and having more understanding, I have come to learn why I went through those times and had those thoughts and feelings.

During those times, I would share with people close to me, simply to have someone to just listen to me and even offer some kind of answer to help me get through those times. Even though I did have a sense of answered questions and somewhat sympathetic friends, which helped, there were underlying issues that I now recognise why I felt I was in those dry places in the first place. Whether you are in that place now or have been in the past, you may find the following insightful and helpful in understanding why you might have been in those places or feeling that you are there right now. I believe what I am about to say is relevant to all of us, at least at some point in our life.

When we read about the nation of Israel coming out of Egypt, God had sent Moses to get them. God was serious and intentional about getting back what was His and seeing that

His most prized possession, His people, were delivered and blessed at the same time. They were under enslavement and harsh conditions for hundreds of years. Enough was enough, and the wheels of God's plan were in motion. It was always in God's heart to free His people and see them prosper in all they do. He wanted to be their God and lead them to a bright and blessed future. So, God made a way where there seemed to be no way. He broke them out of their prison and led them out to freedom.

It was the perfect plan, but there was some resistance and rebellion. The people doubted, argued against the leadership of Moses, and the Lord for that matter, and the people wanted to do their own thing, which wound them up in big trouble. The vast majority, except two from the first generation, only made it to the land God had promised them.

I want to focus on two main points:

1. The journey
2. The location

1. The Journey

Life is a journey. Life is also a discovery. As we read Exodus, we discover that the journey the people of Israel endured for forty years was only about an eleven-day trip. So, what happened? How did an eleven-day trip take forty years to complete? The answer is brief but specific. **'And to whom did He (God) swear that they would not enter His rest, but to those who did not obey? So, we see that they could not enter in because of unbelief.'** - Hebrews 3:18-19.

But let me give you more of the picture so you can understand why things turned out the way they did.

'7 That is why the Holy Spirit says, 'Today when you hear his voice, 8 don't harden your hearts as Israel did when they rebelled when they tested me in the wilderness. 9 There, your ancestors tested and tried my patience, even though they saw my miracles for forty years. 10 So I was angry with them, and I said, 'Their hearts always turn away from me. They refuse to do what I tell them.' 11 So in my anger, I took an oath: 'They will never enter my place of rest.'' 12 Be careful then, dear brothers and sisters. Make sure that your own hearts are not evil and unbelieving, turning you away from the living God. 13 You must warn each other every day, while it is still 'today,' so that none of you will be deceived by sin and hardened against God. 14 For if we are faithful to the end, trusting God just as firmly as when we first believed, we will share in all that belongs to Christ. 15 Remember what it says: 'Today when you hear his voice, don't harden your hearts as Israel did when they rebelled.' 16 And who was it who rebelled against God, even though they heard his voice? Wasn't it the people Moses led out of Egypt? 17 And who made God angry for forty years? Wasn't it the people who sinned, whose corpses lay in the wilderness? 18 And to whom was God speaking when he took an oath that they would never enter his rest? Wasn't it the people who disobeyed him? 19 So we see that because of their unbelief, they were not able to enter his rest.' Hebrews 13:7-19.

The truth is the people of Israel actively chose to turn away from God and go their own way, time and again. They made a conscious decision to reject God, His words and His wisdom.

When they, as a people, and individually, of course, made their choice clear to Moses and God and denied Him a place in their lives, these acts of disobedience of intentionally rebelling against Him was an act of evil in the sight of God. They refused to turn to and trust God. They were fully aware of what they were doing and hence suffered the consequences of their choices. In this way, they did evil in the sight of God, paid the price with their lives, and forfeited their future inheritance.

God had led these people for forty years and did many miracles for them, looked after them, and provided for all their needs. The Garden of Eden event shows that the default condition of the human heart is not to please God but ourselves. So, to truly please God and live for Him, we must humble ourselves continually. But even during those desert experiences, God was still gracious and generous. When we are about ourselves and not for God, we will ultimately find ourselves in similar situations where God does not intend us to go. This does not mean that we are evil people, way off track, or that things are too late to fix. No. It doesn't mean that you are either out of reach of God's goodness or grace. It's not too late for you. Understand God was present for those people through their desert wanderings just as God is with you today. This doesn't mean that I am saying that you are caught up in some terrible sin but that you may be struggling with something that has kept you from entering and receiving His promises for you.

It comes down to how we respond to Him. Are we willing to listen to Him, surrender, and lay aside our own agendas and preconceived ideas? If you identify with these words, then now is the time to get yourself back in the right relationship with Father, turn your heart and thoughts towards Him and decide to live for Him today. Make Jesus your Lord and saviour. Your redeemer and king. Get right with God and enter into your promised land. When you humble yourself before Him, He will lift you up. He wants the best for you today and forever.

One last thought on this point: We must take responsibility for our own choices and not lay blame or responsibility onto anyone else. We can't control what happens outside of our domain of control, but we can take charge of our life and destiny. We don't have to own our sins; Jesus came to take our sins away and bring us to a place where we can see godliness and goodness in all we do. Father God is with you to lead you out of bondage and into bounty.

Also, remember this:

God performed miracles for the people many times. God wants to make a miracle happen in your life too. This is your time to move on and live the life you were created for. Regardless of your past wanderings and seemingly wasted time, though the journey is important, it's where you are headed that matters most to Him. **The journey is temporary, but the destiny is eternal**.

Take some time out now to think and pray if you need to.

2. The Location

The Bible is full of literal and symbolic meanings. When the Bible speaks of Egypt, it refers to the world. In opposition to God. When the people of Israel were coming out of Egypt, it describes God delivering His people out of spiritual bondage, out of darkness, out of enslavement, and out from under oppression. A desert is a barren place. It is also a place of testing. God used this time to test His people to rely and trust on Him. But it was the people who tested God, to their detriment. The people complained about Moses and the Lord. How do you respond to God when you are in a place of challenge, obstacles, or hardship? It is easy to trust and thank God when there is blue sky and sunshine.

When the Israelites came to a place where an oasis was, called Marah, which means unbelieving, bitterness, or grumbling and complaining, it is easy for us to blame God or be negative in our attitude towards Him when things are not going well or according to our own plans. But God uses those 'desert environments' to help shape our trust, faith and dependence upon Him. He uses those times to help shape our character and attitudes.

When we are facing times of distress or feel like complaining, it is in these times we should pray, as this will help our stress levels and put us in a better place emotionally and physically. Desert times are a great opportunity and tool to help change our hearts and strengthen our faith. No matter what situation you are facing right now, God will always provide what you need at that time. God doesn't want to drag us through the desert of tough times; He will if He has to, but they forge and foster our spiritual development. **It's only when you trust God that you obey Him**. And there is fruitfulness and favour that will follow.

I want to finish this part with this important point...

Not everything that happens to us is our fault or doing. God will, sometimes bring or allow events to come into our lives to help shape us, refine us, and take us beyond where we are now in our character and faith. My point is best said with the following verses. **'3 We can rejoice, too, when we run into problems and trials, for we know that they help us develop endurance. 4 And endurance develops strength of character, and character strengthens our confident hope of salvation. 5 And this hope will not lead to disappointment. For we know how dearly God loves us, because he has given us the Holy Spirit to fill our hearts with his love.'** - Romans 5:3-5 It is actually a good thing that we are tested and refined. Father God cannot complete His good work in us if we refuse His opportunities for growth and development. I would encourage you to see new challenges with a new perspective. Because God has a plan, we must be able to handle the small things if we are going to handle the big things, but we grow into that. **Our level of growth is proportional to our level of teachableness.**

He Encourages

God encourages me on a seemingly daily basis. He encourages me by words of Scripture, by his voice when He speaks to my spirit. When I have an overwhelming sense of His grace when I screw up, He still loves me, and I am forgiven. He encourages me when He tells me that He still has a plan for me, even though I think I have wrecked everything. God tells me that I am forgiven, and loved and that I am to move on, to keep moving ahead with things.

In my experience, I realised God's biggest encouragements were present with my biggest failings. Before I got married, I had made several moral and relational failures. And a host of other sins and mistakes also. Please understand me; I had many, many occasions and times for good decisions and successes too. My wins far outweigh my losses. I have done more good than bad, let's say. I have helped more than I have harmed.

Even with those unbridled events, God always kept me accountable, but He also understood that I had areas of my life that required strengthening and shaping. He gave me grace and still does, in areas of my life that went unchecked for a time. Father was always ready to forgive, but He wanted to do so much more than just say, 'keep going'. He wants us to not only live under His goodness and grace, but He also wants us to live in victory, to overcome, to succeed, to triumph, to be strong, to leave certain things behind us, not to be tethered or anchored to our past or with the things that so easily enslave or keep us bound.

God encourages me more than with His extraordinary grace, but He is interested in us having a quality of life but even more, a quality of character, a quality of integrity, a quality of empowerment, and a higher level of personal and spiritual development and perfection. God encourages me because He wants the best in every possible area of my life. Understand God wants us to be physically healthy. God wants us to be spiritually healthy. God wants us to be emotionally healthy. God wants us to be psychologically healthy. God wants us to be socially healthy. God wants us to be financially healthy. God wants us to be intellectually healthy. God wants us to be healthy!

It is Father's will for you to excel in your strengths and to be strengthened in your weaknesses. God is about holistic development and transformation.

Let's get some thoughts down on paper...

What discourages you?

What encourages you?

I am Encouraged when...

I am Discouraged when...

Let's continue...

You may feel encouraged or discouraged depending on your circumstance or news you hear. It is most important to understand where your encouragement or discouragement comes from; feeling one way or another may come from an internal source, not just from an outside source. Your perspective will also influence how you will respond/feel as well.

Now that you've made your two lists, identify the source of your encouragement and discouragement. Where does your main source of one or the other come from? This is important because you will now see who or what you listen to the most and the extent the impact will have on you.

GOD	MYSELF	OTHERS	DEMONIC	CIRCUMSTANCES

Now that you have made your lists, you may have a clearer picture of where your source of encouragement or discouragement comes from.

Again, where does the majority of your Encouragement come from?

Where does the majority of your Discouragement come from?

Whichever you experience, recognise the source. Now that you have recognised the source, you have an advantage over that. See discouragement as an opportunity for a win, a victory, an overcoming moment. Ask the Lord to help you see this discouragement from a different perspective and viewpoint. Change your thinking and declare His word over this situation. God wants to build and lift you up; discouragement, however, intends to bring you down. If it is at all spiritual, tell that demonic influence or power to stop what they are trying to do, and ask them to go in Jesus' name. You do not allow them to have any longer access or influence in your life. Ask the Lord to protect you from further enemy attempts and help you discern if and when they try to bombard you with lies or distorted, discouraging words again.

Another thought...

You can also ask the lord to show you why you begin to feel discouraged about certain words, news or events, or circumstances. Now, like offenses, discouragements will come and go. This is life. But how you respond and deal with discouragement when it hits you will cause a blow to your life or cause you to grow. Ask the Lord to help you with the effects and the severity and extent of the impact things currently have on your life. This will help you to become more resilient and responsive to negative or discouraging occasions. If you feel that your discouragement comes from things you hear, you may need to turn off what you listen to. You may even need to get yourself a new environment to be in. **Build the environment that will build you**. I would also encourage you to, again, pray in the language of the Holy Spirit. There is no substitute for this. It is also worth saying to choose your friends carefully.

As emotional beings, it is normal to feel things all the time; however, our feelings and emotions change and move like shifting desert sands. But we cannot let our emotions or feelings stay in the way or dictate or control our important decisions or responses to situations or upcoming events. Emotions, though, can help us. For example, when we grieve, we may cry. This is a healthy and forward-moving response for healing and recovery to take place. It helps us in dealing with traumatic, hurtful or painful experiences. When we celebrate wins or victories, we have joy and feelings of elation. Every emotion has its place and role in our lives. They enhance our life experience and personal development. They can help protect us too. Anger may be triggered by an injustice you have experienced, witnessed or identified. Your response may lead you to get justice or to end compromised or unbecoming behaviour from others.

Emotions remind us we have the qualities of a God who loves us, for we are made in His image/likeness. Emotions have their usefulness, but they can also work against us if we allow them to. We are emotional beings, but we are also spiritual beings and intellectual beings. When making important decisions, it is good to consider all possible/relevant avenues of assistance; to help us make the better choice for the best possible outcome.

Emotions can either propel us or prevent us from reaching our goals or God-given purpose. We need to manage our emotions every day. This is why one of the fantastic and functional fruits of the Spirit, self-control, is crucial in our daily walk for life and our walk with the Lord. When we allow emotions to take the lead, we almost always run into trouble. When we take charge of our emotions, we take a more forward and leading position, and this helps us to make better choices in the moment. This is when we need the Holy Spirit to lead us and follow His promptings and power to change the course of potential failure and regret.

Ephesians 4:26 says: **'In your anger, do not sin.'** Proverbs 25:28 says: **'Whoever has no rule over his own spirit Is like a city broken down, without walls.'** It's ok to feel angry, but don't stay in that place. Over time there can be physiological and psychological effects that will affect your health. Like stress and high blood pressure, ulcers, higher cortisol levels, tunnel vision, lack of good judgment, social interactions, lack of patience with others, unreasonable behaviour, harsh talk, and so on. Especially in ancient times, the best defense was to have a fortress with high and wide solid walls. They protected and perpetuated a sense of security and safety for the people inside. So, when a city was without its defenses, it was exposed and vulnerable to attack and defeat. Walls can also serve as a mechanism to keep people out of your life.

Isolation is damaging to the individual who keeps walls up for extended periods. The mechanism is that I have been hurt, and I won't let anyone else hurt me again. I won't allow them to do that. The problem is walls do not discern good from the bad. Only the people who govern them. Those who have hurt you are kept from repeating the event, but those same walls can keep those who want to help you out. Therefore, ancient cities had walls, but they also had gates to let people in and out for many reasons. A city that is continually closed off to the outside world cannot continue to exist without supplies, aid or assistance.

At some point, a city must open its gates to let in new people, and new supplies, and let out waste, sickness or disease, or any other potentially harmful entity to be a healthy, functional and productive place. Or, in this case, a healthier and whole you.

His Fatherheart

When I think about God and how He is a father to me. I just can't do Him justice; words are not enough to convey how good He is and how much He loves us unconditionally. The Bible says that God is love. So, when we read 1 Corinthians 13:4-7, it gives us a glimpse of what God is really like.

'4 Love is patient and kind. Love is not jealous or boastful or proud 5 or rude. It does not demand its own way. It is not irritable, and it keeps no record of being wronged. 6 It does not rejoice about injustice but rejoices whenever the truth wins out. 7 Love never gives up, never loses faith, is always hopeful, and endures through every circumstance.'

My own picture of what I would like my dad to look like is one that shows me the ropes, takes me on adventures, protects me, looks after me when I need help, is forgiving, provides, protects, keeps his word, teaches me things, shows me how to handle situations and people, is an influencer, physically and emotionally strong, make decisions, a leader, informed, defends me and steps in for me, calls me out and disciplines and instructs me when I need it, gives me a sense of safety and security, brings me joy, makes me feel special, caring, interested in me and in what I do, gracious, generous, gentle, models manhood, understanding, patient, how to love, judge correctly, give me a sense of responsibility, is assertive, enjoys my company, encourages me, is inspiring, instills values and good morals into me, shows me life skills, is intelligent, practical, has wisdom and experience, a sense of humour, has grit and perseverance, counsels me, goes out of his way, supports me, is about his own business but makes time for me, is hands on.

This sounds like I want the perfect dad; well, heck yeah.

What does your version of a dad that you want look like?

How do you want your father to be?

Our own idea of our kind of dad will look somewhat different to the beholder, but the truth is, Father God is the above list and infinitely more. And while I have mentioned a list like this previously, I have intentionally made this list again as a reminder that no matter how old you are, every boy and girl needs their dad and wishes that they looked something like the above list. I have never felt so significant, fulfilled, happy, joyful, complete, apart, and confident, at home as when I do whenever I spend time with Father God, trusting and following Him.

God takes delight in us; He smiles, looking over us. We read this in Job 33:6 - **'When he prays to God, he will be accepted. And God will receive him with joy and restore him to good standing.'**

Zephaniah 3:17 - **'The Lord your God in your midst, the Mighty One, will save; He will rejoice over you with gladness, He will quiet you with His love, He will rejoice over you with singing.'**

'I will be a Father to you, and you will be my sons and daughters, says the Lord Almighty.' - 2 Corinthians 6:18.

Let me ask two fundamental questions:

1. Why does God want a relationship with you?
2. Why do you want a relationship with God?

Please think about these two for a while. You will, of course, have your own thoughts; here are some of mine.

Firstly, deep down, I was longing for the unconditional love that I didn't have, at least from a father-to-son experience. But I knew deep down that this was something necessary I needed in my life. I craved it. God was the only answer to my emptiness. I desired to be loved and to belong and I found them both from the source. He filled my heart. And He, God, also filled my mind with new and true thoughts. I wanted to understand, and I got that. I needed some answers, and I got those. I needed something outside myself that would provide me with solid satisfaction, meaning and purpose. I wanted to know if this 'God' was true and if He was, I had to make some changes myself. But this would then mean that life was not just for me but for others. It changed my whole perspective and outlook on life. It would also mean that my decisions from the day I met Him until now have all had significant and eternal consequences, good or otherwise. The reason for life and the decisions I now make have new explanations and profound effects.

Secondly, God is complete in Himself and in perfect relationship with the Son and with the Holy Spirit and has been for all eternity. He created the angels for relationship and fellowship. But as we know, He didn't stop there; hence humanity came into being. Why did God create anything? For an oversimplified answer, he wanted to and He could.

Isaiah 43:7 says it better: '**Everyone who is called by My name, Whom I have created for My glory; I have formed him, yes, I have made him.**' God is love, and He wanted to have a creation to be able to know and experience Him. We were made in His image, so we have the markings of love and eternity within us. God, in His unfathomable essence, substance and nature, desired to have and display more of Himself in His creation. Not that He was insecure or narcissistic or needed anything. From nothing, God brought into being the universe, humans and everything else that fills His creation to know Him and to bring Him glory. God wanted people to know His goodness and love firsthand.

God's father-heart is shown to us through His very nature. Any act of goodness, love, forgiveness, compassion, discipline, gentleness, and generosity, amongst many other godly gestures from others, have reflected God's heart and nature.

CHAPTER 15: THE LAST PAGE WITH MY DAD

It was in my early twenties I was in contact with my uncle, and over the years, we talked from time to time over the phone. I knew he was into motorcycles; at that time, I also had my own. So, I decided to visit my uncle. At that point, he and his wife had just had twins, a boy and a girl. I spent some time with them, and I will always have good memories. Many years went by, and I hadn't contacted him, but I later heard that Mick, my dad, was diagnosed that his kidneys were failing. So, I called my uncle and chatted with him, and it was really good. I had always gotten along well with my uncle Brian. I had more to do with him than with Mick, my dad. In that phone call, I had asked him for Mick's phone number.

There was no emotional connection towards Mick, but I realise it was a different story for his other family. All I knew was that he didn't have long to go, possibly months. The only solid connection we had as father and son was a biological one. So, over the following couple of weeks, I considered calling him. Truthfully, though, there were only two reasons I had considered contacting him.

First - I wanted to get some personal resolve and have answers as to why he left. And did he think about us at all over the years? And why didn't you contact us through those years?

Second - As a Christian, I am convinced that when you go from this life into eternity, you simply change location. It is this location you end up in that is most important. You are there forever. So, it was important to me and ultimately for Mick that I knew he had the opportunity to hear every believer's hope in Jesus. Leaving this imperfect and fallen reality is the starting point of entering a perfect and eternal truth. At the very least, I wanted to speak with him about this, then pray for/with him, so that, he could make a decision before it was too late.

Later in August, after thinking and praying about the conversation I was planning to have, I made the call. I was a little nervous as the phone was dialing through. But after he answered, I was ok. The initial and short conversation started with this:

ME: 'Hi, is this Mick?'

MICK: 'Yes, who's this?'

ME: 'It's Brendon.'

MICK: 'Who?'

ME: 'It's Brendon, your son.'

MICK: 'Oh, right." (This wasn't the best start, but it was a start)

ME: 'So how are you feeling?'...

It then went on with him saying the words to me...

'I'm just really glad that you called. I'm so proud of you.'

I had also said to him in that conversation that I was a Christian and that, if he was ok with it, I could pray for him. He said that he would like to know more about my life, and he was even hoping that I had this faith and was willing to share it with him. It was about this time our call was cut short. We spoke for about ten minutes, then got interrupted by a hospital nurse. She was just doing her job. I said I would call him later, and the call ended there.

I didn't get either of the two reasons in that first phone call. So, I had to be patient for the next call. But in the first call, he told me that he was so thankful for me calling him and that he was so proud of me contacting him.

The talk for me was not difficult, but those words would have meant so much more if there had been connection through the years. So even though I was pleased that I had made an effort and was doing what I felt the Lord was leading me to do, there was still no resolve for me yet. I was quite annoyed that it all didn't happen in that call, but I had to trust God that it would happen and that there would be a sense of resolve/closure.

A week later, as I was writing this book, the Lord said that I had to call him right then and there. I asked the Holy Spirit that there would be no interruptions, to guide me and for Him to fill the atmosphere and lead the conversation and that He would also give me the words to speak.

With this second call, I will give you a general gist of what was spoken; otherwise, it would take too long to go through everything said. As expected, Mick was happy with me calling him again, and said it was the perfect time to call. This call went on for just a bit over an hour. In the previous call, he mentioned regret about leaving. But it came across as if he felt no regret for leaving. So, I was a little confused. I needed to get clarity and understanding of what he meant by that. There were only a few important questions I had for him that I wanted to be answered. So, I was quick to ask him. 'So why did you leave?' I figured he owed me at least this much.

The essence of the answer was no surprise to me but informative. I was finally starting to get some closure. He said to me, 'Truthfully, I was afraid.' He said that he was afraid of my mum's family, especially one of her older brothers. There was fear at that point, but there was also another fear that was being expressed as well. He also said that he wasn't running away from mum and us boys but that he was running away from the world.

Not long after all us boys were born, He decided to find some kind of solace for his fears. He was also conveying that they (mum and him) were so young and that they didn't know what they were doing, and there was all of a sudden, this huge responsibility to now look after and provide for five people, himself included. It was also said that he wanted a free life and to do what he wanted to do without limitations or responsibilities. After he left, he found some people who shared similar values and then began to live free and separated from society and responsibility. Drugs were present in his life for a while, but he soon stopped liking that lifestyle.

After heading north of the country, even after years, he said he was paranoid that one of mum's brothers would find him and 'deal' with him. Mick said he had been looking over his shoulder for years, living in a paranoid state.

My next question for him was, 'So did you think about us at all?' He said that he did, and there was a time when we boys were about seven years old. I remember he paid a visit to us. It's amazing what a young child remembers; I told him I remember when he came down and even the car he was driving. It was an old Holden panel van, beige. His response to this question went further, and he said that he had attempted to try and restart a family that had been previously torn apart. There would, be no resolve on my parents' part, no further chance of getting back together.

During the conversation, he had asked me what my life looked like and what my brother's life looked like as well. I shared with him some basic details about their families, what they do, where they live etc. Toward the end of the call, he did ask me when I would be coming up to see him. At the time of this writing, under the Australian border restrictions due to state governments' health and safety orders, there was limited movement from state to state. I said to him that, at least for now, there was no current prospect of leaving the state but possibly at a later stage. He said in response that he would like to hold my hand, look me in the eye and tell me, 'I'm sorry.'

I was okay with the fact that he said this to me during our conversation; if I never spoke with him again after that call, I would be comfortable with this. But if this were to happen, it would be fine. I am a face-to-face person. I'm not too fond of phone calls. I felt that by the end of our talk, I was satisfied with what he said to me, and I had a sense of comfort in my thoughts and heart.

There are probably a hundred things I could have said or should have said, but I like to keep things simple. And for me, I only had a few things I wanted answers for. I felt as though I got those answers. And even though He had his 'reasons,' which not all of them hold any water, I don't have to like or approve of his choices, but I do have to accept that his reality affected my reality, and the past cannot be changed. Only how I deal with things in the now will affect my future.

On my journey, I had unforgiveness to deal with. But at the same time, I had resentment to deal with. I then had to accept what had happened and live with his choices imposed upon me. I didn't want to be dadless, but I had to accept that. And I think this is one of the hardest things I have had to deal with. Indeed, we don't live with the decisions we make; we live with the consequences of those decisions. And in this situation, I had to live with some of the effects of his choices.

Acceptance can be a complicated and difficult road to travel on. Acceptance in one context is not necessarily approving or condoning what happened; it is not even necessarily denying or compromising yourself or your morals, values or principles either. But in this sense, it is starting the process for personal change to where you become settled within yourself, towards others and with God. Unforgiveness, resentment, unwillingness and denial are very real things that can cause us to remain stuck in our lives. They can inhibit and hinder freedom and relationships, and breakthroughs in our life.

All that said, since talking with my dad, I feel like I can now move on. I can keep moving forward into the things in my life and the things of God for my life. This is not to say that there are no residual effects on my life; I am saying that I have a feeling or a sense of not being held back or tethered anymore. I don't feel stuck anymore. Like there is no more hindrance to my personal growth. More than ever now, I can be more fruitful and forward moving in what I am doing for myself and others. I can now have a more genuine and influential impact on others. I also get the feeling of doors and opportunities opening up before me. I know it can seem like a simple and small thing to others, but the floodgates are now open, and God is now able to deliver His awaiting favour and blessing to my personal life and life purpose.

My second reason for contacting my dad was that part of the phone call was unexpectedly a surprise. Though there was rarely contact over the years, I was prompted and led by the Holy Spirit to make the opportunity happen where I was to ask him about his spiritual position, and where he stood with God. At the very least, I wanted to pray with him before ending the call. This was important to me, and I know the Lord wanted me to do this. Mick was quite pleased to hear that I had a personal relationship with God. I had said to him that in my life how God had been a father to me and how He has shaped and is shaping me into the person I am today. I learned from our chat that he had a couple of people in his life who reached out to him over the years to tell him about God and that they were praying for him. In his response, he said he knew God through his devotions, as he put it, and he had peace about his situation too.

You know, God is faithful. I went into this phone call with the view and assumption that I needed to be the Lord's witness to him since he wasn't in an environment where the people around him could not give him that opportunity to hear the gospel truth and to pray for him and share those truths with him. But I was wrong. God had put years earlier into my dad's life a believing couple who displayed Jesus to him and helped him to know and experience God's reality and presence. Even when we may not be in a place where we feel, believe or think that our dad should be given the opportunity to be given grace, love or opportunity for healing, His love for us is far bigger than our sins and mistakes could ever be.

I think of the story of Jonah, where the people of the city of Nineveh were sinning and living godless lifestyles like no one's business, and this was going on year after year. God's judgment was near. Well, Jonah was initially disobedient when he fled; he didn't want to do what the Lord told him to do. He was trying to get away from God and had no accountability. He knew that God was good, showed grace, and loved all people. Jonah knew that if he said to the people, 'Repent!' and the people were to respond to God and heed His call, then God, in his mercy and compassion, would forgive them. Ultimately, God held back His impending judgment for the people to stop their evil ways.

People are ready to receive the message of truth and healing. And even though the situation may not be ideal or even favourable to any party, I had to decide whether I should get on board with God's business or not. Either way, God was interested in the whole thing, and I was to be part of that. As I said, I had no investment in calling my dad and making that connection. But I sensed that God was leading me, and I needed to respond. I didn't want to be judged one day for what I didn't do when I could have made a difference to another when I had the opportune moment.

I want to encourage you if you feel that your situation might seem a little similar to mine. There may be no emotional connection, and there may be no connection at all other than negative, painful memories. But you may just be that person's only lifeline to eternity with God. And this is not limited to family members only. This is not a guilt trip but a faith and obedience trip. Jonah had his own walls he needed to break down before he got on board with God, but he did come through in the end, regardless of how he felt.

Is there someone in your life you know you need to connect with right now? The Holy Spirit might be speaking to you about getting in contact with that other person, but you keep putting it off. If He is moving you, it is for a good reason. This situation may be the very thing that will help you grow and to move on in your own life. If you are at the place where you are willing to go through with what God has placed on your heart, but think that you do not have the words, courage, understanding, patience, grace, love or wisdom. He will help you. He will always equip you for the task at hand.

Throughout our entire life, we must choose to trust God despite our level of understanding, how we feel, or because of our thinking which makes us believe that we are totally inadequate for the job.

'May He equip you with all you need for doing His will? May He produce in you, through the power of Jesus Christ, every good thing that is pleasing to Him.' - Hebrews 13:21.

Doing the Lord's will is good for us. It gives us a sense of meaning, fulfillment, obedience, personal growth, and experience and opens doors for favour and opportunity. It helps us to see and know God in a personal way and to witness firsthand everything He wants to offer. It also causes us to know that we need Him and our dependence on Him is vital for life and wholeness and our overall wellbeing.

When I contacted my dad and spoke with him, I managed to get resolve from that conversation. I'm glad I did because I only had one shot at that opportunity. Afterwhich, it was shortly after I had spoken with him that he passed away. Though I had known that his time was short earlier, I was expecting him to be around for quite some time longer. So, it was initially a bit of a shock when I received the news. My obedient and timely response meant that I could now move on with my life and have some deep healing and closure to my soul. I felt comfortable that I did what I needed to do, and it was timely with no regrets.

To say some final words about this, there is one thought that does come to mind about all this. I sensed about ten days before his passing, I needed to give him a call, but I never did. I was caught up in my busyness of life, and I was fatigued in regard to my health at the time. I felt a gentle prompting to call him by that week's end, but before I knew it, that time had gone and then I got the text message. It wasn't the phone call to make amends or anything like that or to get answers; I already had that conversation. But it was more of a 'see you later, dad, I'll see you in heaven, and we'll catch up again then' type call. It would have been the icing on the cake to everything, as it were. Nevertheless, I have a settledness within me, knowing that I did everything I needed and wanted to do.

Not long after, I caught up with my twin brother and told him about my conversations with Mick. Of course, he had quite a few questions about it, and I answered him as best as I could recall. As a result, I could see how much of an impact it was having upon him. He was saddened by some of the news and past events, but he did say that it was good for him (my brother) to hear it so that he could get some resolve and healing too.

A pivotal moment for healing begins when you recognise and identify the core reasons for your symptoms. What I told him did clear up a lot of questions we both had. He then went on to say how our shared past circumstances had affected his life, of course, very similar to the way it affected me. It explained a lot to him. Fear was the core element for what had happened in our dad's life and his dad's life and before him. Fear just went on down the line. Fear was at the root, but the expression of fear took on many faces. It affected/distorted performance, self-confidence, character development, thinking, self-perception and risk taking.

The list goes on. But right there in the car, we prayed against fear and the impacts and effects of having been without a dad, on each of us. It was a time of breakthrough and healing to varying degrees for both of us, the beginnings of them anyhow. I didn't realise how much of an effect it would have on him, sharing with my brother, so it was very much a God thing I had taken steps to speak with our dad. Now my brother is starting on his journey. Now for us and you too, I may add, the best is yet to come. Better days are ahead.

I want to encourage you that time may be of the essence in your situation. Right now, at this point in your life, you may have valid reasons not to make contact, get resolve or whatever the case may be. This is understandable. For me, I felt that it was my time.

Throughout my life, I have received much grace and still do daily. It was now time to extend that same grace. In this case, it was toward my dad. For you, it may be for your dad. Or it may be for someone else in your life: a brother, a friend, an uncle, or a cousin. God has brought you to this place for good reason, and the knock-on effect will have significant and life-changing implications beyond our thoughts and expectations.

Trust Him and trust Him in the process.

PART 2: ...BUT NOT FATHERLESS

CHAPTER 16: NEW BEGINNINGS AND NEW HORIZONS

No Season Lasts Forever

I know you have heard it said, but it's true. Seasons change; they come and go, and they never last. But this is important because I believe for you on your journey; since you first started reading this book, there has been significant change and progress in your situation, circumstances, and spiritual and emotional development. You are further along now than you ever have been. I would firstly encourage you to keep going. Never quit and believe for the best.

Keep your trust in God and in what He is doing even when you are unsure or do not understand everything that is going on. Trust in His wisdom, response and timing. Father is about bringing permanent change into your life for good. And He is faithful in completing what He began. God didn't stop after day one of creation. He had the vision to fulfill, and He knew that there was more to do before He could finish and bless what He had begun to create.

Winter is typically cold, and summer is usually hot, and we instinctively know when to rug up and sit in front of a warm fire with a hot chocolate, or to go to the beach for a swim, or to cool off under a shady tree with a cold refreshing drink. We know the season and how to respond. So too, does God when He is doing work in our life. At just the right time, He will bring or allow circumstances into our lives to help bring about those needed changes. He knows what to do and when to do those things. And it is in those times we must trust Him. The feelings or circumstances are not always pleasant or comfortable, but He will help us to grow and develop as we allow Him to do good work in us as only He can.

God knows exactly when to plow, plant, tend, water, prune and harvest. God desires us to be fruitful and successful in every area of our life. The fact that you have picked up this book and come this far means that you are not only serious about change but also willing to grow and become the person He intends you to be. He sees the beginning to the end of time, and you are part of that. You play a special and unique role in such a time as this.

A New Start

I want to encourage you to start/keep making 'firsts' in your life. There was a 'first' time picking up the phone, speaking to my dad, and seeing resolve, which helped me move forward.

There was a 'first' in writing a book to help others to work through tough and difficult moments in their life and see them come through and succeed.

There was a 'first' in becoming a dad, and following the example, I was shown by Father God, as nervous and as scared as I was.

There was a 'first' in sharing some of my life with people I didn't know.

There was a 'first' in dealing with issues that kept me from moving forward in my relationship with others and God.

There was a 'first' in working through issues that had me stuck for years, like grief, unforgiveness and resentment.

There was a 'first' when I got on board and agreed with God to let Him lead me through processes of progress for my spiritual, emotional and intellectual development and maturity.

There was a 'first' in seeing God answer my prayer of realising my purpose in life and doing what I really wanted to do, which was significant, meaningful and fulfilling with eternal outcomes.

There was a 'first' in seeing how God not only wanted to use my past but turn around those events for His good and purposes for others' to glean from and benefit. Father wanted me to write this book because I was experienced to share with you and help you traverse your journey for a good outcome and purpose.

You will have many new 'firsts,' 'starts,' or 'beginnings' awaiting you too. Your negatives are to be new positives. Your hardships are to be 'strength ships'. From your situations and circumstances, you will have understandings and insights that others will not have. And God will use you with these. What the enemy meant for evil, God has turned around for good.

'You intended to harm me, but God intended it all for good. He brought me to this position so I could save the lives of many people.' - Genesis 50:20.

When Jesus comes into your life and makes His home within your heart, you become a new creation with a new direction and new hope in this world. You may not like everything about yourself, but you were worth dying for. And now life is worth living because He lives, and He lives in you. When things get tough, hard or discouraging, keep going. Not only for yourself but for the sake of others as well. It only takes one person, one invitation, one moment, one word, and one prayer to change and alter another's life for eternity for their good. When you doubt, get the truth. When you fear, get faith. When you fail, get back up. When you struggle, get help. When you sin, get forgiveness. When you succeed, get humble. When you win, get your praise on. God is on your side, and you and He are the majority.

When you know you have heard from God, don't second guess yourself, and keep moving forward. Stay the course. Others will always have an opinion, but God will always give the truth. When others fail, betray or leave you, God will never leave, forsake, abandon you, or leave you powerless.

He doesn't want to keep you in the dark. He wants to reveal to you personally what to do next and where to go. Living the Christian life is a life of faith. Abraham didn't know where he was going. He just knew that God was speaking to Him, and He said: 'Go!' You see, even when you are not choosing, you're making a decision. So make an intentional one. The Lord is faithful in navigating you through that. **Involve God in everything you do**. Go for it!

PART 2: ...BUT NOT FATHERLESS

God, The Mechanic & Body Repairer of Life

I want you to keep something in mind on your journey of faith and restoration. God is the mechanic, and you are the vehicle. Follow me on this analogy.

People are like vehicles. There are many, many different makes and models. Each is made with a distinct purpose. They have many unique features, shapes, colours, performance abilities, comforts, bells and whistles, sizes, accessories, materials, etc. Furthermore, they may require different fuels and oils and other fluids that are required so the vehicle can operate at optimal performance levels. They also need services at certain times to prevent damage or unnecessary excessive wear. Vehicles go in for serving at specific times to maintain vehicle integrity and performance. This is to perpetuate long-lasting capacities and responsiveness and also keep ongoing costs down to a minimum. There is also the aspect of keeping in step with insurance and warranty.

If a vehicle gets involved in an accident or bingle, there is the body repairer to fix up or replace parts or panels that are no longer workable or simply beyond repair. They even give a new paint job, so you cannot even tell that it was in an accident in the first place, just like brand new. Or it could just be a total restoration job that is being done like an old vehicle just sitting in a garage or outside doing nothing but rusting away, deteriorating over time.

How do you see yourself right now, at this point in your life? What kind of vehicle are you?

Do you see yourself as a new vehicle or one that is beaten up and seemingly beyond repair? Or do you see yourself as something in between the two ends of the scale?

Regardless of where you see/put yourself, we all require a service, a fixup, or a replacement at some point. Going through life, there will be the odd collision, bump, graze, scrape, dent or key-ing. Some damages are our own doing, while other damages comes from others. Either way, a vehicle rarely goes through life without being affected in some way. But to keep things running at their best, they will still periodically require service or replacement of parts. When engines are not firing on all cylinders, the overall performance will be affected. The overall power, speed, fuel economy falls and the general running of the vehicle is impeded. You don't perform as designed or intended. And eventually, you will break down and stop running.

Ok, in our walk with Father God, we must be in constant communication and connection with Him. We constantly require His presence, protection and fresh oil from the Holy Spirit to live a more victorious and fulfilling life. But to also be more effective in service to Him. In our human and imperfect state, we will always revert to entropy. To get worse by default rather than get better. The Spirit of God redeems us, renews us, restores us, rejuvenates us, reinvigorates us, refreshes us, refocuses us, realigns us and reignites us for life and for Him.

When we invest in God, He puts His rewards into us. And like a vehicle, we must get 'serviced' regularly, and have 'parts' of our life restored or replaced to function at our best. This could look like a new location, new friends, job, attitudes or goals. This will mean something specific to you.

Also, God always sees us perfectly regardless of how we see ourselves. If you feel you're a rusted-out old vehicle with no purpose or future, God sees you as a fully restored and renewed vehicle full of new life, hope and purpose. We see ourselves through our own eyes, but God sees us as what we could be through His. An old vehicle restorer sees the end at the beginning, and so does Father God.

Some Last Thoughts

I believe that what we want to see in a dad, or what we would have liked to have seen in our dad, is ultimately what we would like to see in ourselves. And what we would like to see in our children. Even if you do not have kids, you may have a nephew or niece who would like to see those good traits displayed in them. Whichever your situation, Father God wants to see in you what is in Him. We can only become Christlike by having a personal relationship with Him. Be the patient farmer who sows, waters, and waits for the harvest. God will bring the increase over time and make you fruitful.

Don't let failures stop or hinder your walk or growth in Him. Persist in your faith. Persevere in your waiting for Him. Progress through the process. Be persistent in trusting God. When you are in a situation, don't ask the Lord to get you out of it (although this is ok); instead, ask God what you can get from it. Always keep your guard up; you don't want to be blindsided by the enemy or by an old issue that hasn't been dealt with. When temptation comes, go the other way. When you don't know what to pray for, speak in the language of the Holy Spirit. If you feel weak, stay accountable. You are above the task. Be wise about who you befriend and allow into your life and what people speak over you.

Declare God's word in and over your life and get into the word of God every day and regularly connect with other solid and reliable believers. Be open, teachable, and be an encouragement to others. Your example will speak volumes to them. Remember, **you were worth dying for, and Jesus is worth living for.**

You are a man or woman made in God's image, and your best days are ahead of you. God bless you, mighty man of valour and stunning woman of virtue.

STAY STRONG!

ABOUT THE AUTHOR

Brendon Lennon

I started out life in a small town with my mum and two brothers. My elder brother and my twin, of which I am the younger. Our dad left us at a very early age and we had to get on with life without him. Mum made sure we had what we needed, however, there were many struggles and difficulties for her. I didn't grow up in a Christian or religious environment, but at the age of 15, thanks to the goodness and grace of God and some good people, I made a decision to receive and follow Jesus.

Around 18 years of age I moved to the nearby regional city of Albury, and I began working. It was there I spent the next 11 years. During this particular time, I found myself in recurring cycles of unhealthy life patterns; of which later in Melbourne I had personal breakthrough and permanent victory over.

At about the age of 29 I had a growing desire to do some formal study and decided to make the move to Melbourne, Victoria; where I studied at Harvest bible college; subsequently getting my Diploma in Christian Ministry. During that study period I met my wonderful wife, Carmel. And in early 2009 we got married. Carmel and I spent many years being involved in various church ministries.

In 2016 Carmel and I had our son, Isaac. He was our miracle baby, our son of promise. In late 2021 both Carmel and I felt that God was speaking to us to relocate to Bundaberg, Queensland. (It was in this same year also that I reached out to my dad before his passing; from which came much personal resolve and closure.)

At the end of May 2022 Carmel, Isaac and I made the move and are now settling into our new church home at Citicoast Church. We are both excited as to what God has prepared for us in this next chapter of our lives.

www.ingramcontent.com/pod-product-compliance
Lightning Source LLC
Chambersburg PA
CBHW050307010526

44107CB00055B/2144